YES! YOU WILL [
YOUR TEEN WITH ADHD

A PARENT'S JOURNEY TO FIND, LEARN, AND

DEVELOP EFFECTIVE ADHD TOOLS TO HELP

HER TEEN COMMUNICATE AND THRIVE

JAYCEE DONOVAN

Disclaimer Notice:

Please note the information contained within this document is for educational and entertainment purposes only. Every attempt has been made to provide accurate, up-to-date, reliable, and complete information. Readers acknowledge that the author does not render medical or professional advice. The content of this book has been derived from various sources. *This book is not intended as a substitute for the medical advice of phy*sicians. The reader should consult a physician concerning their child's health, particularly any symptoms requiring diagnosis or medical attention. By reading this document, the reader agrees that under no circumstances is the author responsible for any direct or indirect losses incurred due to the information contained within this document.

Contents

Introduction:

Help! My Teen Has ADHD

Looking at old videos on my phone, I saw my daughter. The daughter I remember. The video showed her with her younger brother, simply reviewing and inspecting the toys she had gotten as presents for her birthday. The girl in the video laughed. She smiled. She was entertaining, and she made me smile too. As she laughed with her brother, she modeled and instructed him on how to behave on camera. This was my daughter. My daughter who would one day be diagnosed with ADHD.

Though many children are diagnosed younger, my daughter wasn't diagnosed with ADHD until she was thirteen years old, which is often a confusing enough time for teenagers. When we started our journey, it felt incredibly lonely because I didn't know where to find the answers to all my questions. With experience as a teacher, I knew that there had to be resources out there that could help my daughter — and help me — understand what was happening in our lives.

Since my daughter's diagnosis, I've worked in the classroom with many students affected by their ADHD diagnosis, and I came to learn how prevalent these problems are in children today. Throughout my journey with my daughter (and in the classroom), I developed a support system that led to my daughter's ultimate success, despite her ADHD diagnosis.

The hardest part about her having late-onset ADHD was that every day became such a struggle, both for her and me, and I forgot who my daughter truly was. I forgot that she was funny. I forgot that she loved her brother. I forgot that she had empathy and concern for others. All I saw was an angry person, an anxious person. A girl who could not control her emotions. A girl who could not communicate without spewing negativity. I knew that I made her, that there was good inside her, but I could not remember who she really was at her core. ADHD took that away. It took away her personality.

All I had left to remember the girl I raised was the video that played in front of me as I wondered where she went. Was she still in there somewhere? I had to find out.

If you are reading this book, you likely also have this same conflict. Our stories may differ, but the core experience is the same: You love your child and might feel a little lost right now. You're desperate to understand them and want to do everything possible to help them succeed, grow, and pursue their dreams. Most of all, you want to see them return to the happy child who had fun, loved their family and friends, and felt hopeful about their future.

You are not alone. I know how you feel. I know how disrupting an ADHD diagnosis can be. I know how scary it is when you do not recognize your teen and wonder who this person is. But I'm here to tell my story so you can find purpose in your own. The son or daughter you've loved all these years is still in there, and the tools that will help them return to their happy self are well within reach.

If you picked up this book because you needed a little help understanding your teen, you're in great company. By the end, you will have the tools, resources, and strength you need to achieve exactly that, and you'll also walk away with much more.

You'll find hope for your journey by learning about my story.

When I struggled to help my daughter, I felt an

overwhelming sense of loneliness because I had nobody to guide me through my struggles, answer the questions I wanted to ask and provide the help I couldn't find. I wrote this book with love in my heart for other mothers and fathers who might feel as lost as I did.

Can you do it alone? Certainly! I did. But you wouldn't need to struggle through these challenges by yourself. As you learn about my story, you'll find a connection you seek that will give you the strength you need to get through this.

You'll empower yourself and your teen with coping strategies to deal with the unpredictability of ADHD.

Before I understood what was causing these random changes in my daughter's life, each day held countless obstacles, and normal coping strategies didn't always work for us. That's because there isn't a one-size-fits-all solution for everything. Our children are unique individuals who often need creative approaches to solve the challenges they face as their ADHD symptoms surface.

Throughout this book, we'll explore various coping strategies that helped my daughter and me and discover others backed by scientific and medical research. By the time you finish reading this book, you'll at least have a few tools in your arsenal that will equip you with the help you need to ensure your teen's success.

You'll learn how to communicate with your child's teachers about their ADHD to advocate for their educational success.

One of the biggest obstacles for teenagers with an ADHD diagnosis is finding success in school. Your son or daughter might struggle with testing, homework, paying attention in class, or following complex directions, but you will find help in the school system to address all these challenges and more. As a teacher, I've worked with students of all ages — specifically with those diagnosed with ADHD — and I can walk you through having the most productive conversations with your child's teachers.

However, it's also important to understand that your child's needs may extend beyond the traditional classroom. As a result, I'll also help you explore alternative options to the traditional public school environment if your son or daughter's needs can be met through different methods of learning.

You'll see the light at the end of the tunnel once you understand that life will not always feel this frustrating and complex.

I get it. I've lived through it too. Life with ADHD can often be challenging, frustrating, confusing, and complex because you don't understand what's happening with your child. Your child is experiencing these negative emotions, too, though they may have some challenges communicating that to you.

But life does not have to be like this forever; there is a light at the end of this long, winding tunnel, and this book will provide the light you need to alleviate your frustration.

As you walk along this journey with your son or daughter, you might ask them several questions:

Who Are You, Again?

Your teen's personality has been changing daily, which is when you often notice their personality disappearing right before your eyes. Some days, you might see a shift in their behavior from hour to hour or even minute to minute. Long gone are the days of having a carefree child in your home.

These personality changes can vary from slight moodiness to deep depression, agitation, or anger. During these periods of unpredictability, your son or daughter might scream when they get overwhelmed, or they might laugh at inappropriate times. It can feel extremely frustrating for them — and for you and other family members — to experience these drastic shifts in behavior.

In Chapter 1, we'll explore these challenges so you can understand the underlying causes.

What is Happening to You?

Many who haven't dealt with the reality of ADHD believe it only manifests through hyperactivity or a lack of focus. But here's the truth: There are many more symptoms your son or daughter is likely experiencing, which will vary significantly from another child with ADHD.

Some other symptoms your teen might experience include anxiety, depression, anger, mood swings, extreme happiness, or a lack of self-control. With all these possibilities, it's no wonder you feel like you are dealing with a different person.

In Chapter 2, we will talk about the many symptoms of ADHD so you can recognize when it's affecting your child. (Note: this book section should not be used to diagnose your child. I strongly recommend consulting a medical professional if you have not received a diagnosis.)

Why are You Acting Out?

With all these confusing feelings your teen is experiencing, they will often act out, sometimes leading to potentially dangerous habits, including drinking alcohol, vaping, smoking, or using drugs. While not every child with ADHD experiments with these risky behaviors, it's essential to understand the signs to keep your son or daughter safe.

Teenagers often engage in these types of activities to self-soothe or self-medicate. They think it will make them feel better, but it only worsens things because it can potentially add addiction to their list of challenges.

In Chapter 3, we'll talk about the importance of getting a diagnosis from the doctor to ensure your teen doesn't feel the need to self-medicate their challenges away.

How Can I Help You with School?

It's important to understand you are not alone in this fight to ensure your son or daughter's success. There is support available in the educational system as soon as you have an official diagnosis from your doctor. You can rest assured that your child will have an entire team behind them at school: a psychologist, social worker, principal, and all their teachers. This support team will create a learning plan customized to their specific needs, requiring excellent communication between you, your teen, and their support team at school.

In Chapter 4, I'll help you navigate through the school system to get your son or daughter the support they need to find success in their education.

Are Your Friends a Good Influence on You?

Teenagers need friends and positive social life to develop into healthy adults later in life, so the people they spend their time with now can make or break their well-being. Peer pressure is still a very real danger for kids today, and this can often lead to those dangerous self-soothing habits if their group of friends is not a good influence on them. You want the best for your son or daughter, so you want to ensure their friends support them, not lead them down a dangerous path.

In Chapter 5, we'll explore positive friendships for your

teen, so you can ensure they stay safe, healthy, and happy as you help them cope with their ADHD diagnosis.

How Can I Help You Find Treatment?

Finding proven ADHD treatment options is paramount to helping your teen with their diagnosis. Treatment options for others might not always work for your son or daughter, so you must understand what medical treatments can help your child. Some patients find great relief with medication, while others might need other ways to manage their symptoms. (Note: I won't advocate for or against medication, as that is a personal decision based on your child's situation. But I will briefly discuss it as an option that has worked for some patients.)

In Chapter 6, I'll help you explore the existing different proven treatment options, including behavioral therapy, psychosocial treatments, medication, and activity-based therapy.

Can I Talk to You About ADHD?

My daughter didn't hide what she was doing to cope with

ADHD in her unique way; she wanted my help. However, she didn't know how to tell me what she needed. Communication will be one of your most essential tools throughout your journey to help your son or daughter with their disorder.

In Chapter 7, we'll dive deep into the importance of positive communication and how it can help you alleviate your frustrations and confusion about how ADHD is changing your lives.

What Will Your Future Hold?

New treatment options that yield promising results for teenagers with ADHD continue to become available. I find this very encouraging because traditional treatment methods don't always work for every patient. The medical industry has brought many innovations that offer exciting alternatives to medication and therapy, including non-stimulant medications, exercise-driven therapy, medical devices, and even prescriptive video games.

In Chapter 8, I'll close by showing you some alternative forms of treatment for coping with ADHD that will provide more hope for the future of your son or daughter's ADHD.

* * *

These were all questions I asked internally when first presented with my daughter's diagnosis. I designed this book as a journey through all those answers I desperately needed to find. It is set up in such a way that you don't have to read it from point A to point B – simply find the question that's weighing on your mind and start reading.

By picking up this book, you have made the first positive step toward realizing your hopes and dreams for your child's future. You may have started this journey alone, but I'll be with you the whole time, telling you my story, showing you helpful strategies and coping mechanisms, and directing you to resources you might not have known existed.

For you, it might not be a video that tells a story about who your son or daughter used to be. It could be a photo or a treasured memory from the past that you ache to be reunited with. Whatever the image is, I want you to know it is possible to experience that joy again. An ADHD diagnosis might cause some setbacks in you and your teen's lives, but those precious moments from childhood are far from over.

Are you ready to learn more about your ADHD teenager? It

all starts with the first question.

Chapter 1:

Who Are You Again?

By now, you might have noticed the drastic difference in your son or daughter's personality. These new changes aren't simply normal teenage behavior; it's something much different, something you weren't prepared for.

As a parent, I felt so troubled that I could no longer describe my teen's innate personality or her emotions from moment to moment, as it was constantly changing. I remembered her humor, curiosity, and empathy as a small child, but those traits seemed like a blur now. She went from being full of joy and enthusiasm to full of anger and frustration.

Sometimes, she was so impatient with the simplest of tasks. Even worse, if somebody tried to help her with anything, she would yell and scream at the person to leave her alone. Her moods varied drastically. She would be agitated one minute and then silly and laugh inappropriately the next.

But she wasn't the only one who changed after her ADHD

diagnosis. I also went through the growing pains of her evolving personality.

The Difficulty of Everyday Life for Teenagers with ADHD

School and Homework

One of the biggest challenges with ADHD is your teenager's involvement in school and doing homework — to the point that things can seem practically impossible. At first, it started with notifications from my daughter's teachers. Sometimes, it would be a missing assignment, or maybe she did poorly on a test. Initially, the challenges didn't overwhelm us, but they quickly became something that felt impossible to navigate.

Every day when she would come home from school, I'd ask about homework. She either wouldn't have any, or she would forget. My daughter forgot many things when it came to school, and for a while, I thought this was code for "I don't feel like doing my homework." To someone who hasn't experienced ADHD, this feels like an excuse or a flat-out lie. As parents of ADHD teenagers, we must understand that forgetfulness goes much deeper than a child who simply can't stand to do their homework.

We can explore why this happens in your ADHD child by learning more about executive functioning. Hundreds—or even thousands—of times a day, your brain performs one of two functions: some don't require conscious thought (normal bodily functions, reflexes, laughter, etc.), and then those that need some planning. This second type of function our brain does is called executive functioning. *Psychology Today* explains that the following are executive functions:[1]

- Self-awareness

- Inhibition

- Verbal and nonverbal working memory

- Emotional regulation

- Motivational regulation

- Planning

- Problem-solving

---

[1] Executive Function. (n.d.). *Psychology Today*. Retrieved February 18, 2023, from https://www.psychologytoday.com/us/basics/executive-function.

ADHD is a disorder of executive functioning, so you can imagine how hard it is for your teen to start and finish their homework. Their executive functioning is not as easily accessible as a non-ADHD brain.

Socializing

One of the reasons socializing becomes difficult for teenagers with ADHD depends on one of the primary symptoms of ADHD — the tendency to get easily distracted. This side effect manifests itself easily when they try to engage in conversations at social events. From my personal experience with late on-set ADHD, when a teenager with ADHD is having a conversation, one of three things happens:

1. They often interrupt their peers in conversation.

    Though this behavior gets misinterpreted as being rude or unkind, it stems from what I discussed earlier in the chapter during our discussion of executive functioning. When conversing with one of their friends, they tend to interrupt the conversation; otherwise, they are afraid they might forget the important thing they had to say. It doesn't matter how important the information is; teenagers with

ADHD struggle with short-term memory loss. When they interrupt someone, it's their way of ensuring they don't let their friends down by not participating in the conversation.

2. They can get easily distracted from a conversation, requiring their friends to repeat what they said.

    Again, this often gets misinterpreted by their friends as being disrespectful, but their lack of focus is something they really can't control. Either an internal thought or worry is plaguing their mind, or something is happening nearby that causes them to lose focus. Their friends might think they are bored with the conversation, but this distraction is not voluntary. It is something that happens naturally in their minds.

3. They might withdraw completely from conversations to spare their friends' feelings.

    It can feel frustrating when people judge you for how you interact in conversation. This is especially true for teenagers who also have to contend with bullying, peer pressure, and other societal expectations. Their friends might think it is because they are not interested in the conversation, but it is grounded in a genuine feeling of empathy.

Communicating with Parents

Ask any teenager, and they'll tell you their parents simply don't understand them. If you reflect on your adolescent years, you will remember feeling this way a time or two. And this is just for teenagers without disordered brains; it is even more challenging for teenagers with ADHD.

Your son or daughter with ADHD wants to communicate with you, but they do not know how. I cannot tell you how often I would beg my daughter to talk to me about what was going on, only to get a door slammed in my face, or she would scream at me to leave her alone. For a mother with a close relationship with her daughter, I almost cannot find the words to explain how heartbreaking it feels to get that sort of reaction from her. It almost feels like she is trying to rip my heart out through my chest. I understand now that it is not her fault, but in the past, I had moments where I honestly thought she hated me. I thought I had lost my best friend.

If you are experiencing moments like this today, please understand that it will not be like this forever. Together, you will find the tools that work to break those walls that ADHD built around you.

Friendships

If your son or daughter struggles to build or maintain friendships, they are not the only ones. Research done by the Child Mind Institute, a leading mental health care facility in New York City, reveals that about half of the teenagers diagnosed with ADHD have problems making friends or maintaining their current friendships.[2]

Your teen needs to understand that it is not because they have done something wrong, but it, unfortunately, does mean they will need to work harder to improve the friendships they have.

The Child Mind Institute recommends coaching your teenager to help them improve their social skills with their friends:[3]

---

[2] Miller, Caroline. (2023, January 9). Social Issues for Kids With Learning Problems. Child Mind Institute. https://childmind.org/article/social-challenges-kids-learning-problems/.

[3] Helping Girls With ADHD Make Friends. (2021, August 19). Child Mind Institute. https://childmind.org/article/helping-girls-with-adhd-make-friends/.

- Emphasize taking turns when spending time with your son or daughter and explain how they can repeat this with their friends at school, church, or outside the home.

- Give your teen several examples of resolving conflict, especially if they tend to be impulsive. Role-playing could be an excellent way for them to practice this before they do it without you.

- Create scripts that walk your teen through how to have positive social interactions if their socializing skills are lacking. (Note: this could be a useful tool to get from their therapist if you need additional resources.)

- Remember that your child sees you as a role model, so it helps to exhibit positive social behavior when they are around so they can learn how to master their social life as you do.

Anger and ADHD

My daughter and I fought plenty of times due to the unpredictability of ADHD. Both of us expressing anger about what we could not control led to hurtful things said on either side of our arguments. I know now that ADHD was to blame for these fights, not her because I didn't understand how the disorder affected her.

Though it is not your son or daughter's fault, raising a teenager with ADHD can be stressful because you often feel you must compensate for their lack of social, behavioral, and communication skills. Some days, you are happy to carry this burden because you want to do everything possible to ensure your teenager's happiness. However, you likely have some dark days when you simply feel like you do not have the energy to lift yourself up, let alone your child dealing with ADHD.

Your son or daughter is not the only one experiencing anger as you both adjust to their new diagnosis. There have been times you feel that anger, too, as you battle with understanding why your teen struggles with homework, chores, hygiene, and more. In the beginning, it often feels like it is a choice for them. This misconception leads to numerous fights and regular tension between your child and you.

Admitting this anger and frustration is not easy because we

are talking about the child you have raised from the time they were born. Mothers are supposed to be nurturing, but just like our children, we are only human. When things feel overwhelming, we struggle with managing our intense emotions too.

I want you to understand that it is not your fault either. You are both dealing with an unpredictable situation, and you will grapple with feelings of confusion, frustration, intense anxiety, and anger to a certain degree. These emotions are natural responses to the chaos that ADHD creates in your lives.

Much scientific research has been done on how ADHD-fueled anger affects adolescents. One such study led by Ilina Singh of the BIOS Research Centre in London explained that the anger that stems from ADHD is different from the anger we understand:

"Anger" in relation to ADHD does not refer to an experience of feeling outraged in response to a real or imagined injustice. Instead, "anger" refers to self-control struggles in aggressive situations. A poorly controlled short-fuse is probably the most common understanding of ADHD that we encountered.[4]

One of the students in their study spoke about an incident with a classmate diagnosed with ADHD. He said that if somebody teases him, he can't get it out of his head. "He jumps on people's backs and squeezes the back of their necks."[5]

Explained like this, we can start to understand that this anger is not something your teen can control. It takes hold of them, squeezes them mentally, and doesn't seem to give up until they act out their anger.

But what can we do about it?

Children and Adults with Attention-Deficit/Hyperactivity Disorder (CHADD), an organization that offers support and resources for patients with ADHD, offers four strategies to help your teen with their emotional regulation:[6]

---

[4] Singh, I. (2011). A disorder of anger and aggression: children's perspectives on attention deficit/hyperactivity disorder in the UK. *Social science & medicine (1982)*, 73(6), 889–896. https://doi.org/10.1016/j.socscimed.2011.03.049.

[5] Ibid.

[6] Breaux, Rosanna, PhD. (2020). Emotional Regulation in Teens with ADHD. CHADD. https://chadd.org/adhd-news/adhd-news-caregivers/emotion-regulation-in-teens-with-adhd/.

1. Develop a list of coping skills.

   CHADD recommends that you both keep a list of coping skills to help with emotional regulation. They offer suggestions, such as "talking to a friend or parent, exercising, listening to music, drawing or writing in a journal, taking a shower or bath, taking time to calm down, taking deep breaths, or practicing mindfulness."

2. Acknowledge your teen's emotions.

   With my daughter, our best conversations happened when we both slowed down enough to listen and acknowledge how each other felt. Listening is a technique that is imperative when establishing an effective communication pattern. Sometimes it is easy to talk but harder to listen, especially when emotions are involved. Our communication has dramatically improved by just listening to each other.

3. Promote the introduction of healthy habits into your teen's lifestyle.

   You can focus on nutrition, better sleep habits, and introducing more activity into your son or daughter's life. I know it made a tremendous difference for my daughter and me when we both made healthy changes in our lives.

4. Manage your own stress, anxiety, and anger.

   Both you and your teen are on this path together, and it is essential to acknowledge that your emotional well-being needs to be nurtured too. CHADD believes that "ensuring that you are in a good emotional state makes it more likely that you will respond in supportive and helpful ways."

Age of Diagnosis

The path to finding the answers you need will vary depending on when your teen received their diagnosis. Suppose your teen was diagnosed with late-onset ADHD as my daughter did. In that case, you are likely to have many more challenges in the teenage years because it can often be confusing to distinguish between normal teenage behavior and ADHD symptoms.

The Scapegoat of "Normal" Teenage Behavior

When I first noticed the changes in my daughter, I did not realize they pointed to something much bigger than what her peers were dealing with. Whenever a teenager acts out, has mood swings, or talks back, it is normal for us to misinterpret it as everyday teenage behavior. After all, puberty, peer pressure, and societal expectations can often make our children become unpredictable at times. This is when ADHD gets the best of us—when we do not know our teen is struggling with it.

The first hurdle we had to overcome was realizing that it is not easy to diagnose late-onset ADHD. One of the primary reasons for this is that the *Diagnostic and Statistical Manual of Mental Disorders* (DSM), which contains the medical criteria for diagnosing mental disorders, created the list of symptoms for ADHD for children twelve and under. In fact, in addition to the ADHD symptoms that we'll explore in the next chapter, a patient must also meet the following conditions:[7]

- Several inattentive or hyperactive-impulsive symptoms were present before age 12 years.

- Several symptoms are present in two or more

[7] American Psychiatric Association. (2013). *Diagnostic and Statistical Manual of Mental Disorders (5th ed.)*. https://doi.org/10.1176/appi. books.9780890425596.

settings, such as at home, school, work; with friends or relatives; or in other activities.

- There is clear evidence that the symptoms interfere with or reduce the quality of the social, school, or work functioning.

- The symptoms are not better explained by another mental disorder (such as mood, anxiety, dissociative, or personality disorders). The symptoms do not happen only during schizophrenia or another psychotic disorder.

The highlighted portion would present a huge challenge if your son or daughter's symptoms did not present themselves until after age twelve.

ADHD Symptoms Extend Beyond Restlessness

Most people know that hyperactivity and restlessness are significant symptoms of ADHD; after all, it is right there in the name of the disorder. That is one of the reasons my daughter's diagnosis came as such a surprise. Though she had moments where she felt and acted restless, the other symptoms—the ones that often do not get as much publicity—screamed much louder in her mind.

My daughter experienced the following symptoms before she got her ADHD diagnosis:

- **Intense Anxiety**

  In normal situations, anxiety is typically a reaction to stress. You feel anxious if you suddenly find yourself in a dangerous or scary situation, like getting in a car accident or becoming a victim of a crime. Increased heart rate. All-consuming fear. Sweat all over your body. Your body sends these signals to motivate you to either fight or run away. It is quite a powerful feeling.

  However, in teenagers with ADHD, anxiety is a much bigger problem, and it all goes back to that executive functioning I talked about earlier. When teens cannot cope with their lacking executive functioning skills, they become consumed with worry, and intense anxiety takes over.[8] Because ADHD affects your teen's executive functioning several times

---

[8] Saline, Sharon, Psy.D. (2022, March 31). Anxiety in Teens with ADHD. *ADDitude.* https://www.additudemag.com/anxiety-in-teens-adhd-reframing-skills/.

throughout the day, this can often cause them to be anxious for hours daily.

- **Depression**

    Returning to the idea of your son or daughter's challenging executive function, you can imagine the toll that dysfunction takes on their mood. Suppose they are not managing their anxiety well. In that case, they will likely experience depressive episodes, which will cause them to withdraw from social life and family activities and affect their performance in school.

    Depression steals away their motivation to achieve anything as it reminds them of how hopeless things in their lives have become. This side effect of ADHD can become destructive and even life-threatening, so it is essential to keep the lines of communication open if you suspect your teen is depressed. (Note: you should also always keep in mind that it is important to notify their therapist if you feel they are in danger.)

- **Anger**

    We have already talked quite a bit about how ADHD can make your teen angry and how it differs from the anger you are used to experiencing. So, I will simply reiterate that anger is a prevalent emotion that can get out of control in teenagers with ADHD if they struggle to regulate their emotions.

- **Lack of Self-Control**

Psychology Today defines self-control as "the ability to manage one's impulses, emotions, and behaviors to achieve long-term goals."[9] And guess what manages your teen's self-control? Yes, that's right—their executive functioning. As you are likely starting to figure out by now, this part of your child's brain affects many of their emotions, often negatively.

This dysfunction lies at the center of the unpredictability of ADHD, and the side effects can affect multiple aspects of their life. But now that you better understand what it is and how it informs your son or daughter's ADHD symptoms, you are in a better place to help them reclaim their self-control.

- **Drug and Alcohol Abuse**

---

[9] Self-Control. (n.d.). *Psychology Today*. Accessed February 19, 2023, from https://www.psychologytoday.com/us/basics/self-control.

When all these symptoms remain unchecked or unnoticed, sometimes disastrous results ensue. I can say this because I experienced it with my daughter when she started vaping, drinking alcohol, and doing drugs. However, with us, it was a cry for help. My daughter wasn't hiding the fact that she was engaging in these risky behaviors. She wanted my help but did not know how to ask for it.

If your teen is self-medicating, too, it is time to take action and open the lines of communication before these destructive symptoms worsen.

The symptoms I noticed in my daughter, and the accompanying behaviors that were a daily part of our lives, were cries for help. She was trying to tell me something was wrong in her own way, and I used those signals to get the help we needed. Your daughter or son may not be exhibiting these exact symptoms because there are more we have not talked about yet. (We will explore those other symptoms in the next chapter.)

The Explosion of Late-Onset ADHD

My daughter experienced all these symptoms before we

finally had answers to the ever-so-important question: *Who are you again?* The answer came by way of her diagnosis — late-onset ADHD. As I mentioned before, late-onset ADHD is a complex diagnosis because the diagnostic criteria require the symptoms to be present in early childhood.

But what about our children who exhibit ADHD symptoms late in the game? Our stories are important, too, and they need to be told because so many other teenagers out there need a diagnosis to get the help they need.

When left untreated, we often don't realize there is a bigger problem until all those underlying symptoms come out to play together. It explodes like a bomb in our lives, threatening to destroy the happy child we have come to know and love.

When this explosion came into our lives, we were unprepared for the damage it would do to my daughter and our family. Late-onset ADHD acted like a wedge between us, creating chaos in its wake. I was unprepared for how it would affect our lives; none of us were.

My daughter's diagnosis caught me off guard because everything I knew about raising children would not work for her situation. Once her diagnosis had its hooks in our family, I knew I had to throw away my expectations. I had to do something different if I was ever going to be able to understand who she was.

I refused to believe the beautiful girl from the video was gone; that was where our journey started.

Chapter 2:

What Is Happening To You?

I first noticed a difference in my child during sixth grade. At first, I noticed that she could never sit still. She would walk around the house on her cell phone, sometimes bouncing a tennis ball, for hours. Then the difficulties at school started. My daughter said she would ask to go to the bathroom multiple times during classes so that she could walk around. It seemed like her restlessness had taken over her life, often making it difficult to perform everyday tasks.

I mentioned this to her doctor during her annual visit with the pediatrician. She responded that she didn't have ADHD because she would have demonstrated symptoms early in childhood. She asked if her teachers ever mentioned anything to me about their concerns, and when I said, "no," the doctor said we should give her a cup of coffee in the morning. She claimed the caffeine would help her focus. In our case, coffee was not the solution.

It didn't make sense. I wondered, *How can my daughter have all the symptoms yet not qualify because of her age?* After all, she was experiencing the same problems a younger child with an ADHD diagnosis would experience. These new symptoms affected all areas of her life, and we needed help.

In my journey to understand what was happening to my daughter, I focused on what I could learn from her symptoms.

Symptoms Commonly Associated with ADHD

Whenever anyone hears the term "ADHD," they imagine certain behaviors: restlessness and hyperactivity. The *DSM* outlines the following behaviors that are associated with restlessness and/or hyperactivity:[10]

- Often fidgets with or taps hands or feet or squirms in seat.

- Often leaves seat in situations where remaining seated is expected.

---

[10] American Psychiatric Association. (2013). *Diagnostic and Statistical Manual of Mental Disorders (5th ed.).* https://doi.org/10.1176/appi.books.9780890425596.

- Often runs about or climbs in situations that are not appropriate (adolescents or adults may be limited to feeling restless).

- Often unable to play or take part in leisure activities quietly.

- Is often "on the go," acting as if "driven by a motor."

- Often talks excessively.

- Often blurts out an answer before a question has been completed.

- Often has trouble waiting their turn.

- Often interrupts or intrudes on others (e.g., butts into conversations or games).

The criteria for this portion of diagnostic guidelines (there are two groups of symptoms, with a third set of conditions required for a diagnosis) state these requirements: "Six or more symptoms of hyperactivity-impulsivity for children up to age 16 years, or five or more for adolescents age 17 years and older and adults; symptoms of hyperactivity-impulsivity have been present for at least six months to the extent that is disruptive and inappropriate for the person's developmental level."[11]

Then there is the other set of symptoms that have their own requirements. This other group of symptoms relates to something often associated with ADHD: lack of focus. If your son or daughter struggles with focusing, you might notice the following behaviors:[12]

- Often fails to pay close attention to details or makes careless mistakes in schoolwork, work, or other activities.

- Often has trouble holding attention on tasks or play activities.

- Often does not seem to listen when spoken to directly.

- Often does not follow through on instructions and fails to finish schoolwork, chores, or duties in the workplace (e.g., loses focus, side-tracked).

- Often has trouble organizing tasks and activities.

- Often avoids, dislikes, or is reluctant to do tasks that

---

[11] Ibid.

[12] Ibid.

require mental effort over a long period of time (such as schoolwork or homework).

- Often loses things necessary for tasks and activities (e.g., school materials, pencils, books, tools, wallets, keys, paperwork, eyeglasses, mobile telephones).

- Is often easily distracted.

- Is often forgetful in daily activities.

The following requirements must be met for this set of symptoms: "Six or more symptoms of inattention for children up to 16 years, or five or more for adolescents age 17 years and older and adults; symptoms of inattention have been present for at least six months, and they are inappropriate for developmental level."[13]

When I look at all the above symptoms, my head spins. My daughter experienced most (if not all) of the symptoms at some point when we were struggling to get an ADHD diagnosis. The doctor's "prescription" of morning coffee would never be a viable solution for my daughter, and I knew it. After all, caffeine is not a miracle cure-all, and in

---

[13] Ibid.

some cases, it can worsen things.

The coffee suggestion certainly could not help my daughter's lack of self-control. This symptom is another common presentation of ADHD, though it is not explicitly mentioned in the *DSM*. In my estimation, the reason for this is that the lack of self-control is responsible for all these symptoms that lie at the foundation of ADHD as a whole. And there is a very important reason for this.

For those of us without ADHD, self-control comes easy. We understand the consequences of doing—or not doing—something which motivates us to complete a task or accomplish a bigger goal. However, for our teenagers with ADHD, the consequences are different. They also have to contend with what seems more like an anti-consequence when remaining focused on certain things.

Dr. Sam Goldstein, a pediatric neuropsychologist who specializes in child development, explains this paradox:

Kids with ADHD have trouble paying attention in only some situations. These are situations in which they must bring online increased self-control and effort to remain attentive. Such situations are repetitive, effortful, uninteresting, and usually not of the child's choosing. When these situations do not provide immediate, frequent, predictable, and meaningful payoffs or rewards for completion, children with ADHD struggle even more.[14]

This is why your son or daughter can play a video game for hours—or some other activity that holds their attention—yet, they struggle to work on homework for thirty minutes. With my daughter, rewards would not motivate her to prioritize her schoolwork. It is not that she did not want to work towards receiving a reward or chose to ignore her school obligations because she simply did not like it. The problem was that her ADHD brain made it impossible for her to concentrate on it because it did not give her an immediate and frequent reward. Our children's brains simply have to work much harder than ours to accomplish goals that do not challenge other kids much.

The Other Symptoms My Daughter Experienced

It is essential to understand that these are not the only

---

[14] Goldstein, Sam, Ph.D. (n.d.). What Is the Relationship Between ADHD and Self-Control? LD Online. Accessed February 23, 2023, from https://www.ldonline.org/ld-topics/behavior-social-skills/what-relationship-between-adhd-and-self-control.

symptoms our children experience; ADHD encompasses many more negative effects. Sometimes, these other symptoms are so predominant that they convince you that another problem might be causing all these changes. But, if you want to understand what is happening to your son or daughter, you must also understand the full picture of ADHD.

Lack of Anger Management

In the previous chapter, I talked a little bit about the relationship between anger and self-control when teenagers find themselves in situations that appear aggressive (this can be either real or imagined). This ADHD-fueled anger can cause problems in your son or daughter's social, work, school, and family life, especially when dealing with people who lack an understanding of where this anger comes from and why it's hard to control.

That reason? Your teen with ADHD cannot control their emotions as well as you do. Though it is not a part of the current diagnostic criteria, this aspect of ADHD has been recognized as an effect of ADHD even before those diagnostic criteria were created. Back then, ADHD was known as "minimal brain dysfunction." The medical professionals of the day recognized that "aspects of negative emotionality" informed how this dysfunction affected the brain.[15] This tells us that there is much more to ADHD than meets the eye. You and I both know that our teenagers struggle with more than hyperactivity, lack of self-control, and inattentiveness. But you also know it is pretty complex; many of these other symptoms are connected at a high level. They work together to make everyday life more difficult for your son or daughter, so you must understand how they connect and present themselves in different aspects of your teen's life.

Anxiety

It is hard to sit back and witness how anxiety rules your child's life. If you have not experienced intense anxiety yourself, consider yourself lucky. Anxiety, especially in teens, is the voice that makes their worst fears true. It leads them to believe at least some of the following things about themselves:

- There is something very wrong with me.

---

[15] Nigg, Joel, Ph.D. (2022, July, 11). Anger Issues and ADHD. *ADDitude.* https://www.additudemag.com/anger-issues-adhd-emotional-dysregulation/.

- I will never be able to do this.

- I am not good enough to achieve my goals.

- My ADHD makes me a bad person.

- Nobody likes me or wants to be my friend.

- People cannot stand to be around me because of my ADHD.

- I am stupid. (My daughter says this sentence several times a week.)

- I am worthless.

- I am unattractive.

- I am too fat (or too skinny).

Almost everyone experiences this type of negative self-talk at some point in their lives, but for teenagers with ADHD, it tends to take over and control nearly everything. Dealing with this level of anxiety is hard enough for people without ADHD, so you can imagine how paralyzed your son or daughter might feel about dealing with these types of feelings several times throughout the day.

These thought patterns tend to worsen their ADHD because the deck is already stacked so high against them. Your teen already suffers from the inability to achieve long-term goals because of their disordered executive functions. Still, when you add these in, it makes it impossible for them to care about trying.

After all, if your daughter or son is already convinced this negative self-talk is true, what reason do they have to fight against it? They will go down the path of least resistance, which does not always include positive behaviors. It often leads to extended periods in front of a computer or video game system, too much cell phone use, or life-threatening addictions they think will self-medicate those thoughts away. But, once that activity is done, those hurtful thoughts will likely return. It is a never-ending cycle.

Depression

Normal teens experience slight depression or sadness when they get rejected, break up with their boyfriend or girlfriend, do poorly on a test, or disagree with a friend or family member. But the type of depression I am talking about has nothing to do with that type of sadness. Sadness, when comparing it to clinical depression, can go away once enough time passes that allow you to cope with the loss. With clinical depression, there is no source. It just shows up one day like an unwanted visitor who refuses to leave.

Depression in your ADHD teen often comes "out of the blue" for no logical reason whatsoever. It feels like a huge weight hovering over them, and even the easiest of tasks become difficult. For instance, I have seen my daughter struggle to shower or clean her room for days because of her depression. It zaps away her energy to live a healthy, happy, and functional life. And if left unrecognized or untreated, it can lead to destructive behaviors and even suicidal ideation or suicidal thoughts.

Did you know that up to 38 percent of teenagers with ADHD also experience symptoms of major depression? Medical studies have even indicated that teens with ADHD and major depression suffer more dysfunction than patients without comorbidity.[16]

Think about your teen struggling with both disorders — ADHD and depression — for a moment. Your son or daughter already deals with a dysfunction that makes it harder to engage in everyday tasks because of the issues with executive functioning. Then depression comes along

---

[16] Turgay, A., & Ansari, R. (2006). Major Depression with ADHD: In Children and Adolescents. Psychiatry (Edgmont (Pa. : Township)), 3(4), 20–32.

and holds them, hostage, making it impossible to do anything at all, sometimes even the things they love.

In these conditions, it is not hard to understand why more dysfunction exists when the two disorders are present. ADHD and depression are essentially forging a partnership that creates chaos and unpredictability wherever they go.

Lack of Positive Communication Skills

So far, we have talked about quite a few symptoms that work together to make your daughter or son's life exponentially harder. However, these challenges are all happening beneath the surface—and most of the time without your knowledge. What makes it even worse is the fact that your teen does not know how to talk to you about it.

You might ask them questions like, "How can I help you get this done?" But your child does not have the slightest idea about how to answer that open-ended question. It is too broad and confusing for them to tackle. If they knew how to answer that question, they would not have as many challenges getting things done.

Their lack of communication skills also extends beyond that. From our discussion about the clinical diagnostic criteria for

ADHD, earlier in this chapter, a few symptoms highlighted their other communication problems.

The following clinical symptoms speak to those problems:[17]

- **Often talks excessively.**

  This symptom often causes problems in school and social situations where people have certain expectations about how their son or daughter should act. Especially in school, it can be problematic, often causing them to get in trouble for disrupting the class.

- **Often blurts out an answer before a question has been completed.**

  Many of their teachers might think this behavior originates from having a rude personality, but it stems from your teen's struggles with short-term memory issues. They are simply afraid they will forget an answer to a question, and their anxiety forces them to answer before it is appropriate, so they will not be judged for their forgetfulness.

---

[17] American Psychiatric Association. (2013). *Diagnostic and Statistical Manual of Mental Disorders (5th ed.).* https://doi.org/10.1176/appi.books.9780890425596.

- **Often interrupts or intrudes on others (e.g., butts into conversations or games).**

  This behavior also relates to their challenges with short-term memory. The entire time somebody else speaks, they wait for them to stop before they forget what they have to say. It is essential to understand your child does not do this to be disrespectful; they do this because they want to be a part of the conversation in their own way.

Inability to Relax and Insomnia

One thing that affects my daughter's life tremendously is her inability to relax. With ADHD, teenagers deal with this because of two reasons: 1) Energy boosts often come at night, making it more challenging for them to relax their minds and fall asleep; 2) Stimulant-based medication can also make sleeping and/or relaxing more difficult because the active ingredient keeps them awake for longer periods.

We have tried natural remedies and relaxation techniques, but those do not always offer the best solution. Your teen's psychiatrist can prescribe medications to help with this if they feel it is necessary, but sometimes, it is simply the nature of the beast we have to deal with as parents of teenagers with ADHD.

Even more than the sleep problems is the fact that they can cause ADHD symptoms to worsen during the day, according to Dr. Michael Breus, a sleep medicine expert, and clinical psychologist.[18] Like you and I, your son or daughter needs restful sleep for their brains to function best the next day. It is already hard enough for them with their disordered executive function, so you can imagine how this cyclical nature of ADHD can worsen things exponentially.

Dr. Breus also identifies the other sleep problems he typically sees in children and adolescents with ADHD:[19]

- **Obstructive sleep apnea (OSA).** Individuals with OSA experience difficulties breathing during sleep due to blockages in their airways. ADHD commonly presents alongside this condition.

- **Bed-wetting.** Wetting the bed is common among children with ADHD, though it's unclear why.

- **Restless legs syndrome (RLS) and periodic limb**

---

[18] Breus, Michael, Ph.D. (2022, December 13). ADHD and Sleep. The Sleep Doctor. https://thesleepdoctor.com/mental-health/adhd-and-sleep/.

[19] Ibid.

movement disorder (PLMD). Kids diagnosed with ADHD experience RLS and PLMD more frequently than other children. For children with ADHD and RLS, the ADHD symptoms tend to be more severe than in kids with just ADHD.

- **Bruxism.** Sleep-related bruxism is teeth grinding or clenching the jaw while sleeping. Teeth grinding occurs more frequently in kids who have ADHD. (I have also noticed that the stimulants in common ADHD medication can also worsen this problem.)

So, if your child is experiencing these symptoms, please know that you are not alone. Other teenagers with ADHD experience these problems too.

Unable to Tolerate Life's Frustrations

In all aspects of their lives, ADHD makes it challenging for teenagers to accomplish their goals. This feels incredibly frustrating because there is nothing your daughter or son can do to change their diagnosis. It often leads to various negative emotions, including anger and irritability, confusion, frustration, sadness, and low self-esteem.

In my daughter, this frustration came out in her bursts of anger: screaming, slamming doors, and lashing out at anyone who questioned her behavior. When you have other children in the family, they often don't understand why their sister or brother behaves this way, and it can send shockwaves through your family.

With this and all the other symptoms we have discussed in this chapter, your teen with ADHD simply need some coping techniques that serve as an intervention to those feelings of frustration and anger.

PsychCentral offers some great suggestions for how to deal with all these ADHD symptoms:[20]

- **Give [your child] time and space to strategize:** Developing and executing strategies are challenging for teenagers with ADHD, so it requires practice and understanding as we help them work through their frustrations. Not every strategy we tried worked for us, but we found one that worked well with some experimentation.

- **Create an ADHD tool kit:** Your son or daughter will have many frustrations in different areas of their

[20] Juby, Bethany, PsyD. (2021, August 17). Tips for Coping with ADHD. https://psychcentral.com/adhd/best-tips-for-coping-with-adhd.

lives, and you will not always be there to help them when they arise. PsychCentral suggests including lists, timers, and alarms as part of this tool kit to help them focus on what needs to be done. Something I have noticed that works really well for my daughter is giving her a time limit to achieve something. This holds them accountable for their task and motivates them to do it. These strategies are especially useful when your teen begins to use them on his/her own.

- **Relax and decompress:** This strategy is easier said than done—at least, it has been for us because my daughter has challenges relaxing her mind. But you can have your teen try breathing exercises to start out, which should give them space to calm their minds and slow down their thought process.

- **Take care of [the] body:** This sounds incredibly simple, but it is not always automatic for children struggling with ADHD. You can check in with them to ensure they are eating, sleeping as well as they can, staying hydrated, and getting the proper amount of exercise. These strategies will obviously not cure their ADHD, but they will help them prepare their minds for the day's goals.

- **Build [their] self-esteem:** Having self-esteem is one of the biggest challenges we have struggled with because my daughter's anxiety often causes her to question her ability to do certain things. Listen to what your son or daughter says about themselves and talk to them about it if it takes a negative turn.

- **Ask for help:** This coping technique can be challenging if your daughter or son struggles with anxiety because it often makes them feel like a burden if they need too much help throughout the day. But asking for help is not a weakness — it is actually a strength. I try to model this behavior for my daughter, so she understands that not everyone is perfect. We all need a little help sometimes.

All these symptoms can harm your teen's life, but it does not have to be a sentence. Once we understand that our children simply need different strategies and ways to cope with their ADHD brains, we can begin to help them return to that happy child we remember from all those years ago.

Your child is still in there; you simply need to do some work to bring them back out.

Chapter 3:

Why Are You Acting Out?

When my daughter did not get a proper diagnosis, she attempted to self-soothe and do whatever she thought would make her feel better. These behaviors included dangerous and life-threatening activities such as vaping, drinking alcohol, and self-harm. Because she had such a hard time relaxing and falling asleep, she looked everywhere for anything that would solve her problems, no matter what they were. She asked "friends" for advice or talked to strangers online. Because she was overwhelmed with the symptoms, she could not make healthy choices for herself.

Addiction

Teenagers rarely think they will have problems when they use substances, especially ones considered legal for adults to imbibe. But their bodies are still developing at a young age, and they can have a toxic effect on them. Beyond that, my daughter was experiencing ADHD symptoms. On top of the intoxicating effect of the substances her friends and the internet "prescribed," she also had other natural emotional impairments because of her lack of executive functioning.

Normal stimulants for most people, such as nicotine, alcohol, and caffeine, would have a reverse effect on her. But, once she started using these things to calm down, her condition worsened. They might have seemed fun to try at first, but she quickly learned she did not want them anymore; she needed them. Despite their adverse effects on her, her brain demanded more and more.

We were in a dangerous spot. Without the diagnosis my daughter desperately needed, she took matters into her own hands in ways I thought she could not possibly understand. Her behaviors could derail her life — and even endanger it. I knew that I had to do something to help her.

The problem caused by addiction in your ADHD teenager all starts with their ability to access the dopamine in their brains. Commonly known as a feel-good hormone, dopamine is also responsible for other functions in the brain, most notably executive function, which we have already determined is problematic for teenagers with ADHD. Mental Health America (MHA), a non-profit organization that promotes mental health for overall well-being, further explains that "whenever you need to do something, your brain triggers a little release of dopamine to motivate you to do that thing."[21]

Many mental disorders are caused by a low or nonexistent supply of dopamine. However, with ADHD, it is a bit more complicated than that. Your teen actually has a problem with dopamine transporters, which are responsible for eliminating dopamine. They have more of these transporters than a non-disordered brain that removes dopamine too quickly, making the hormone inaccessible to someone with ADHD.[22] With this happening inside their brains, it is no wonder they have so many challenges with executive functioning.

Because of this, my daughter craved more dopamine to promote relaxation in her brain. She was terrorized by

---

[21] What is Dopamine? (n.d.) Mental Health America. Accessed on February 25, 2023, from https://mhanational.org/what-dopamine.

[22] Legg, Timothy, J., PhD, PsyD. (2019, June 18). What is the link between ADHD and dopamine? *Medical News Today.* https://www.medicalnewstoday.com/articles/325499.

sleepless nights caused by racing thoughts and physical restlessness, so she did what she thought might give her a little reprieve from these symptoms. In some ways, she was not wrong. Nicotine, alcohol, and drugs *do* increase dopamine levels, but it comes at a cost.

That cost is addiction.

At first, using these substances felt harmless to my daughter because they gave her exactly what she needed to relax and live her life without feeling frustrated all day. However, the more dopamine her brain got, the more it depended on it to function, turning her brief reprieve into an addiction that created more chaos than the ADHD symptoms themselves.

If your child has not experimented with these substances, there is no guarantee that they will. This is merely one of the paths your son or daughter can take if their symptoms are left untreated. With my daughter, it seemed as though it stemmed from a combination of several things: her frustrations, untreated ADHD, "friends" giving her bad advice, and an inability to communicate what she needed. All these things became the perfect storm for her addictions.

I did not discover my daughter's addictive behavior by accident; in fact, I think she wanted me to discover that she was stepping into dangerous territory. She wanted me to know that she felt she had nowhere else to go but down. Discovering this motivated me in a big way to fight for her, to fight for her diagnosis.

In fact, that is why you picked up this book and why you are still reading right now. You came prepared to fight for your daughter. You came prepared to fight for your son.

Now that we are in this fight together, it could be helpful to know what some of the signs and symptoms of addiction might look like in your teen:[23]

- Frequent changing of friends

- New friends you disapprove of

- Excuses made for odd or unusual behavior

- Withdrawal from activities with family or friends

- Frequent breaking of rules or ignoring responsibilities

- Getting home past curfew regularly

---

[23] Ali, S., Mouton, C. P., Jabeen, S., Ofoemezie, E. K., Bailey, R. K., Shahid, M., & Zeng, Q. (2011). Early detection of illicit drug use in teenagers. *Innovations in clinical neuroscience, 8*(12), 24–28.

- Unusual or violent behavior

- Impaired judgment

- Talkative when normally quiet

- Truancy in school

- Grades dropping significantly

- Apathy, poor morale, low productivity, lack of self-control, aggressive behavior, difficult temperament, and poor interactions with family members, friends, teachers, and others in the community

- Dressing inappropriately or wearing inappropriate makeup

- Acting manipulative or secretive

- Going from laid back to dramatic behavior

- Threats of violence or uncharacteristic behavior (quitting school, running away, destroying property, etc.)

- Bloodshot eyes or dilated pupils

- Sudden weight loss (or weight gain)

- Easily fatigued

Of course, even if your teen exhibits these symptoms, it will not always mean they are using drugs, drinking alcohol, or smoking. They are merely red flags that can signal something more is happening. You might have even noticed that some of these symptoms echo the behaviors of a teenager with ADHD. Use your best judgment, open up a line of positive communication with your daughter or son, and seek professional help if you feel you need it. Nobody knows your child better than you, and only you can get them the support they need if something out of the ordinary is taking place.

Self-Harm

Equally disturbing and dangerous is the threat of self-harm, which can come in many forms. The one you are most likely familiar with is cutting because it gets the most attention in mainstream media. One of my daughter's "friends" suggested that she cut because even just a small cut would take her mind off the racing thoughts in her brain. In other words, she would focus temporarily on her physical pain, not the mental one.

Self-harm encompasses anything your teenager might do

that is meant to cause them physical pain. In addition to cutting, my daughter would burn herself with matches and hit herself repeatedly on her leg. Though not our experience, eating disorders can also become apparent. My daughter felt this overwhelming urge to hurt herself, and this was one of the ways it manifested. For teenagers with untreated ADHD, it is pretty easy for them to feel overwhelmed. That can be dangerous when they feel they have no recourse but to hurt themselves.

Whenever she felt like she needed to hurt herself, she would feel an overflow of negative emotions: sadness, anger, desperation, confusion, heartbreak, and/or rejection. With many teens who also self-harm, these emotions hit them all at once, and they do not quite know how to handle them. It almost feels like a strategic attack, causing their brains to overload. The pain they inflict distracts them from what is going on inside their minds. Even if short-lived, it releases them from all those confusing emotions rolling through them.

I did not discover this behavior immediately; she had been doing it for months since the warning signs showed. And, by then, it had become such a habit to her that it was incredibly hard to stop it. With eating disorders, it can be even more dangerous because you do not always see the signs early enough. Sometimes, such as with eating disorders, the bruises and scars remain on the inside. My daughter's cuts and burns were very small. Nothing on the outside told me what was going on with my child. If your son or daughter is self-harming, this is also probably true for them.

It is essential to understand that self-harm does not always appear so obvious in physical ways. Their injuries might even seem minor, but even if they don't look serious, self-harm is a major concern because it can lead to major injuries, life-threatening health issues, or suicide attempts.

If your daughter or son is engaging in self-harm, you might see the following emotional signs:[24]

- Sudden behavior changes such as becoming withdrawn, moody, or irritable

- Being sad or depressed, crying

- Changes in eating or sleeping habits

---

[24] Warning Signs of Self-Harm. (n.d.) Ball State University. Accessed on February 28, 2023, from https://www.bsu.edu/campuslife/healthsafety/campus-safety/campussafetyhandbook/warningsignsofselfharm.

- Increased use of alcohol and/or drugs

- Sudden changes in appearance, especially the neglect of appearance

- Restlessness and agitation

- Overreacting to criticism or being overly self-critical

- Being unable to recover from a loss, ongoing and overwhelming feelings of grief

- Dropping out of activities and becoming more isolated and withdrawn

- Experiencing radical personality or behavioral changes, including increasingly dangerous risk-taking behavior or sudden improvement in behavior

- Making final arrangements and giving things away

- Threatening to commit suicide and openly talking about death, not being wanted or needed, or not being around

Additionally, you might see the following physical signs

with a self-injuring teenager:[25]

- Several or frequent cuts, scratches, bruises, bite marks, or other wounds

- Several scars, often in patterns or on the same area of the body

- Excessive rubbing of an area to make it burn

- Keeping sharp objects nearby, such as in their bedroom, bathroom, or personal belongings

- Constantly wearing long sleeves or pants, especially in hot weather

- Frequent accidental injuries

Medical professionals do not consider this a mental illness, but they do consider it a side effect of various mental disorders. The reason this is so prevalent in mentally ill youth today, according to a study published by *The Journal of Crisis Intervention and Suicide Prevention*, is due to their lack

---

[25] Signs and Risk Factors of Self-Harm in Youth. (2022, January 28). Camber Children's Mental Health. https://www.cambermental health.org/2022/01/28/signs-and-risks-of-self-harm-in-youth/.

of healthy coping skills.[26]

Like our discussion above about addiction, it should not surprise you that some of the symptoms here also mention things that could indicate untreated ADHD. Many disorders in the *DSM* have a lot of shared symptoms — symptoms like the ones that come with both addiction and self-harm.

Here is the bottom line for teenagers who self-harm or self-injure: these behaviors are cries for help pointing to a much bigger problem. I have been through this with my daughter, so I understand how lonely and helpless both of you are feeling. The answers to my daughter's problems did not come easy; we both had to work hard to find a better path forward. I recommend starting off by having an open-minded conversation with your teen. When you talk to them about the ways they are acting out, I recommend keeping the following things in mind:

- Your teenager needs to know that you will always offer a safe space for them. Whether that means listening, offering healthier solutions, or arranging

[26] Guerreiro, D. F., Figueira, M. L., Cruz, D., & Sampaio, D. (2015). Coping strategies in adolescents who self-harm. *Crisis, 36*(1), 31–37. https://doi.org/10.1027/0227-5910/a000289.

for them to meet with their therapist, they need to know you are there for them.

- More than anything, your son or daughter needs you to listen without passing judgment. Adolescence is a hard enough experience *without* adding ADHD into the mix. You can make it easier by being a great listener.

- You need to prepare yourself to hear the hard things, whether that means talking about drugs and alcohol, self-harming, or some other negative experience, they need help coping with. They are already confused about what is happening to them; they need a parent with a strong capacity to listen and react appropriately.

- When your child acts out, do not be afraid to recognize and calmly discuss it. Problems do not get solved easily by sweeping them under the rug, and your teen needs you to be courageous enough to be their truth-teller. This will allow them to respond in a safe environment that values healthy solutions.

- It is okay to acknowledge that you do not know how to handle addiction or self-harm. Ask for help when needed so your daughter or son also sees this as a healthy way to solve problems.

Now more than ever is the time to ramp yourself up to advocate harder for your child. While they might not realize it, they are endangering their lives to find a solution to the problems ADHD is causing.

Social Isolation

Parents of teenagers with ADHD struggle with the idea that they have lost their son or daughter to the chaos the disorder causes in their lives. I struggled with that, too, because I wanted to see the determined and happy little girl smiling, playing, and making us all laugh. That was what she loved to do. This metaphorical disappearing act, however, is nothing compared to the literal one that physically steals your child from your everyday life.

With my daughter, the change was subtle. Maybe she would hide in her room for an hour or two longer than expected to avoid the pressure of others' reactions to her ADHD symptoms. Not everyone understands what happens when you first deal with a diagnosis—or trying to get one. Someone in the home might misinterpret those symptoms as bad habits or behaviors, so some off-hand comment about how your child is acting could be quite hurtful. Not only does this happen at home, but it also happens at school. Thus, instead of only feeling judged by family members, your teen could also be dealing with problems at school too. This creates a deep feeling of shame and worsens social isolation.

You know what "they" say, "kids can be cruel." Their peers at school will latch onto any perceived difference, and whether they mean it to be cruel or not, your son or daughter gets their feelings hurt. This can be even more dangerous for a teen with ADHD because they already feel insecure about the changes they are experiencing. Anything else that singles them out can push them into a deep, dark corner, and though it might feel safe to withdraw at first, it can be unhealthy for a developing adolescent.

The American Psychological Association (APA) advises that extreme loneliness and isolation can have some adverse effects:[27]

---

[27] Novotney, Amy. (2019, May). The risks of social isolation. Monitor on Psychology. https://www.apa.org/monitor/2019/05/ce-corner- isolat ion.

- Depression

  Teenagers — and especially teenagers with ADHD — are already at high risk for depression, as discussed earlier. However, social isolation can make this even more intense for your daughter or son. When they isolate themselves socially, they have no one to lean on for support, only themselves. As that loneliness ramps up, they retreat more into their isolation.

- Poor sleep quality

  Again, this is already an issue for your daughter or son because of their ADHD symptoms and/or diagnosis. But, if socially isolating themselves makes their sleep quality even worse, even more health problems can ensue if it prevents them from sleeping entirely. Sleep — and excellent quality sleep — is as essential as our basic bodily functions, so anything that makes this impossible is extremely unhealthy for your child.

- Impaired executive function

  Like the previous two adverse effects of social isolation we have discussed, this is also a primary symptom of ADHD. Your daughter or son needs their executive functioning to do well in school, at work if they have an after-school job, and at home. Impairing this further can have a detrimental effect on every aspect of their life.

- Accelerated cognitive decline

Your teenager needs their cognitive functions because they are partly responsible for every intellectual activity they perform: thinking, weighing decisions, studying, learning new information, etc. Social isolation attacks these abilities, which, ironically, is what could pull them straight out of their isolation.

- Poor cardiovascular function

If your child is isolating themselves, it is likely their activity level has turned rather sedentary. They spend a lot of time sitting at their desk or on the couch, or they might even be lying in bed for hours. This lack of activity has a negative effect on their blood pressure, which will affect the health of their cardiovascular functions. This should not be a concern for your daughter or son at such a young age because they have so much life left to live.

No matter how you look at it, all three ways of "acting out" — addiction, self-harm, and social isolation — are the emotional and physical consequences of untreated ADHD. They are the ways in which your daughter or son has disappeared from their normal lives, and the longer they remove themselves, the more dangerous it can get for them. As a parent of a teenager with ADHD, their ultimate safety and well-being are in your hands, and you naturally want to do everything you can to help them.

This is what I ultimately did to help my daughter:

1. First and foremost, I advocated for her ultimate diagnosis of late-onset ADHD. Because my daughter was vulnerable, I knew we would not be able to solve her emotional crisis until I could use my voice to amplify hers. It was a long and stressful process, but it was worth it in the end because I never gave up on the fight. And, make no mistake about it...that is what this is: a fight for our children's happiness and success.

2. I went to all the medical professionals armed with research, facts about my daughter's experience, and questions I needed answered. Even if I had to write

them down to remember them, I wanted the doctors and therapists to know about everything we went through so they could get a full picture of what was going on in our lives.

3. And, no matter what, I showered my daughter with love, understanding, and patience. They need this from us because we are their protectors, and they are up against enough obstacles in the outside world. I made our home a safe place to express and communicate ideas, thoughts, and fears.

The road will not be easy if you are still on your way to finding solutions for your daughter or son, but you will get there. You will find pillars of success that work well for both you and your child, and you will find a way to make the detrimental effects of ADHD much better. Once you do, the "acting out" will lessen, and you will be well on your way to finding the happy child inside. And, yes, that child still exists!

Chapter 4:

How Can I Help You with School?

There is an excellent support team for you and your teen at school that deals with the conflicts presented by ADHD, even if it is late onset. A learning plan must be implemented immediately to guarantee your teen's success. This can be initiated and recommended by the school psychologist, who helps put a team in place, typically including a social worker, counselor, teachers, and principal.

My daughter did not begin experiencing conflicts in school until the second half of seventh grade. Up until then, the only comment I received from teachers was that she was "so quiet." When in full-blown "ADHD" mode, however, she couldn't stop talking. She would talk to friends, ask the teachers off-topic questions, and chat with people walking by the classroom door. She became "checked out" and did not do homework or study for tests (which actually caused intense anxiety). She was angry and often in fights with friends at school. She would ask to go see the nurse often. I would get daily phone calls and emails from the school reporting her "negative behavior" or asking me to pick her up from the nurse.

The reality is, however, your child does want to do well. With overwhelming restlessness and a lack of self-control, my teen struggled to keep up. And, despite what the teachers assumed based on her behavior, she cared about school. It is frustrating when behavior and performance do not indicate this. Her teachers thought she didn't care, she was not trying, and she simply wanted to be a troublemaker. With my teen, this triggered deep depression and anxiety, which was overwhelming.

The great news is that this can all be turned around with communication and talking to whoever you possibly can about your child and the conflicts a teen can encounter when having ADHD.

How ADHD Manifests at School

I was immune to my daughter's ADHD symptoms when they first started manifesting in our home. One of the reasons why this was so challenging for us was because it was easy to explain them away as "normal" teenage behavior. After all, the percentage of teenagers who actually enjoy academics is much lower than the ones who do not. And one thing was certainly true for my daughter: She hated school with a passion, and that hatred for school manifested in many ways.

Inability to Focus

One of the hallmarks of ADHD, especially in teenagers, is that focusing on tasks is incredibly hard. Our children need as much focus as they can muster in an educational environment, so ADHD is already setting them up for potential failure. I would receive calls from my daughter's teachers telling me she would instead draw or talk to her classmates than pay attention to the current lesson. When this happened, learning what she needed to know was practically impossible.

Our children are smart—there is no doubt about that. However, their lack of focus makes them appear as though they are not because they would instead do anything else than the actual schoolwork they are required to do. My daughter did not want to fail out of her grade, but her inability to focus made getting an education much more challenging than it was for her classmates.

Teenagers without ADHD understand the consequences of not paying attention in class. They know that if they do not do what their teacher asks of them, they might not pass their grade. And nobody—especially not your teen with ADHD—wants to repeat a grade.

Falling Behind in Schoolwork

And what do you suppose happens when your son or daughter finds it hard to focus in school? They fall behind in their schoolwork. In a traditional educational environment, this is a huge problem because they only have a limited amount of time to catch up on their missed assignments. When they do not beat the clock that is constantly ticking away, they get a zero on that assignment, which makes their average lower exponentially with each missing assignment.

One of the things about a teenager's ADHD brain that makes this worse is the part of their executive functioning that helps them remember tasks they need to complete. That means that in addition to remembering the end result of the task—the completed assignment—they also need to remember all the steps they need to take to finish it well. That is a huge deck stacked up against any teenager with

ADHD.

I cannot tell you how often my daughter said, "I forgot," whenever I asked her about an assignment. At first, it felt like a little white lie she was telling because she simply did not want to do her homework. But, as those perceived excuses stacked up, I knew there had to be a bigger problem at play.

This problem made me feel completely useless in this situation because I couldn't be with her in every class, so I would know what she needed to do for homework. But I wanted to find a way to help her somehow; I just did not know what form that help should take.

Anxiety

Every morning was a fight at home because my daughter wanted more than anything to avoid school. This constant battle in her mind created intense anxiety regarding school days. And our children spend *a lot* of time in a classroom, as the law requires. It will vary based on where you live, but where we live; the requirement is 900 hours per year in K–6 and 990 hours per year up to the twelfth grade. Some states in the U.S. have even greater requirements.

Our children should not be consumed with anxiety for

almost 1,000 hours in a given school year. It takes a toll on their emotional and physical well-being, things we are responsible for as we raise our daughters and sons.

That anxiety can take many forms:

- Social challenges with their peers

- Taking tests

- Fear of not passing the year

- Pressure to give the right answer when called on

- Challenging math problems

- Forgetting crucial material needed for homework and tests

And when I asked my daughter what caused her anxiety in school, she said, "School in general." So, for her, absolutely everything caused her to be consumed with anxiety. That is quite a lot of pressure for an adolescent to go through.

It does not matter that many of their peers might not have these same problems. Your son or daughter is an individual with unique challenges that cause them stress and anxiety every day at school.

Lack of Communication with Teachers

When my daughter was in the process of getting a diagnosis, one of her teachers was very active in helping move that along. However, she also had to manage other students struggling with ADHD symptoms. With ADHD being one of the most common developmental disorders diagnosed in children, this was not a surprise to me. But it still affected the teacher as she worked to balance her attention between the students in need and the others. This fact of being a teacher is not anyone's fault; it is simply a reality of the job.

These teachers work very closely with our children and are often the first to notice their cognitive struggles. However, with my daughter, she only knew that she did not want to be in class because of all the pent-up anxiety it caused. This created some challenges in communication between her and her teacher. She could not communicate her issues adequately, leading to many misunderstandings in the classroom.

Without that diagnosis, though, it was hard for me to set my daughter up for success in school. We have so many hopes and dreams for our children at the beginning of their lives, and it can feel heartbreaking when we see them struggling through the stress, anxiety, and obstacles they face in school.

Lack of Self-Control in the Classroom

With all these challenges our ADHD teenagers are up against in school, it should be no surprise that things can easily get out of control in the classroom. It is not enough to remind them of the expectations because they already know what you and their teachers expect of them. They simply lack the tools they need to make that happen.

One thing that posed a unique challenge for my daughter was her lack of self-control. In this regard, her development lagged behind her classmates with no ADHD diagnosis. They could focus, do their schoolwork, and communicate well with their teachers. Her impaired executive functioning misdirected her attention constantly, and she did not know how to change that.

I knew we needed help, and I worked hard to connect with the school system to get that help.

The Major Players in ADHD Conflict Resolution at School

My daughter needed an entire team at school if she was ever

going to find success there, and with my background in education, I knew there were systems in place to help us. If your teenager is still struggling in school, it is essential to understand that the teachers, mental health professionals, and principals want your child to be successful too. You are not alone in this fight.

School Psychologist

The school psychologist will be essential to you and your child when you get the ADHD diagnosis and throughout your son or daughter's entire education. Their help does not stop once you define the root of the problem.

But first, you have to start with the problems your teen is having in school. In the beginning, you will likely receive a lot of communication from teachers once any issues arise in the classroom or their schoolwork. Combined with your efforts with medical and outside mental health professionals, you will also work with the school psychologist to determine what is causing their problems in school.

In addition to any tests those outside medical professionals might have done, the school psychologist will also perform some behavioral and psychological tests—with your permission, of course. This testing will help them determine if there are any mental health issues or learning disabilities holding your child back from their success.

This process is extremely important because it will set the foundation for the services and accommodations the psychologist will ultimately recommend based on the results of those tests. They will use the 504 Plan (or IEP), which we will discuss later in this chapter, to create a plan for your son or daughter that equips them with all the tools they need to find success in the classroom.

After this plan is set in place, it is essential to understand that it is not set in stone. If any additional testing is needed later on in their education, they will conduct them, then adjust the 504 Plan if your child needs more or different accommodations.

However, their work is not done there. The school psychologist will also coordinate with your son or daughter's teachers to help with any behavioral challenges they might experience in the classroom.

School Counselor

While the school psychologist takes responsibility for investigating the causes of your child's problems in school, the school counselor focuses on how they can help them achieve their goals. They communicate with the students one on one more regularly than the school psychologist does, so they likely have more intimate knowledge of your son or daughter's daily struggles.

This flow of communication is extremely important because your child's needs will likely change from week to week, especially as their work throughout the school year gets more challenging. This also equips them well to contribute to the yearly review required for the 504 Plan since they, along with your child's teachers, will be more familiar with those daily challenges that could help shape the accommodations made in the plan.

Another important role the school counselor plays is maintaining great communication with teachers and parents. At this stage in the game, your son or daughter likely has at least a handful of teachers, and they probably have different challenges in each of those classes. The counselor will be able to balance and manage those unique challenges and coordinate a plan for the bigger picture with everyone involved.

They invest heavily in your child's success in school, but that does not stop at helping them navigate through classes, schoolwork, and behavioral expectations. It also extends well into the future, especially as your daughter or son gets older and starts thinking about their hopes and dreams for a successful life.

There is a future for your child, and it does not have to include one without college or any additional schooling because of how challenging it has been for them to get through school. Maintain an open relationship with the school guidance counselor, who will be able to guide you through all the tools and resources needed to build toward, in particular, post-secondary success. A guidance counselor can help find extracurricular activities to develop specific skills and interests and offer great advice on defining future goals and expectations and how to get there.

Every child's path will be unique, and that does not always include advanced education. The school counselor understands this and will help in whatever way they can to set your son or daughter up to achieve their goals and pursue their dreams.

Teachers

Like the school counselors, your teen's teachers are at the

foundation of what will eventually make them successful throughout their education. Through their daily interaction with your child, they get a bird's eye view of how they interact with their peers and other teachers, behave in their daily schoolwork and on tests, and perform at their best.

They also have a unique perspective that can help you better serve your teen's diagnosis because they have a front-row seat to how your son or daughter's executive functioning fails them. This is one of the reasons why teachers are so integral to the diagnosis process. Because of their daily interaction with your child, they can communicate useful information that guides medical professionals in making important decisions about their care.

When I was considering different areas of treatment for ADHD, including medication, I relied heavily on communication with my daughter's teachers to evaluate the frequency of ADHD symptoms in the classroom and her overall performance. My daughter struggles with her working memory, meaning she struggles to recall prior learning. She needs classroom strategies that will help with this. How can the teacher assist with this?

Our conversations also included performance updates on

homework and tests and behavioral tendencies: Was she awake and alert? Was she on task? Was she participating in class discussions? Was she speaking to friends instead of staying on task? Quite frankly, medication was our last-ditch effort to improve her school life. I wanted to know that it was necessary, effective, and making a positive difference.

Individualized Educational Plan (IEP) or 504 Plan

So far, the team we have discussed represents the perfect situation with the right variables in place to ensure your child is as successful as they can be in school. However, not everyone has the same experience in the educational system or with their mental health. That is why there are laws and regulations in place that ensure your son or daughter gets the help they need at school. However, they cannot get that help without a proper diagnosis.

Once you have that diagnosis, you can start working with the school psychologist to set up an IEP or 504 Plan that will explain what your teenager needs to even the playing field at school. The school psychologist will review information from outside medical professionals, teachers, counselors, parents, and your child, to form a definite plan about the help they need to succeed at school.

Here are some possible accommodations you might see in a 504 Plan for an ADHD student:

- Quiet classrooms to do their homework

  In some schools, this special classroom is called a resource room, where your child will work with a "resource teacher." This highly educated special educator helps your son or daughter with their challenges and other students with varying mental illnesses who also have accommodations outlined in their IEP.

- Special accommodations for taking tests

  Many teenagers with ADHD experience test-taking anxiety, especially if there is a time limit on those tests. Some accommodations will give them extra time to complete the test or a quiet space free of distractions to set them up for a better test-taking experience.

- Seating arrangements

  Some students with ADHD will benefit from sitting closer to the teacher, making it easier for them to concentrate on the lectures or lessons. Or perhaps they might benefit from having additional space between them and other classmates if those classmates cause your child to get more distracted.

ADDitude also recommends these other possible accommodations that cover the extent of an ADHD diagnosis:[28]

- Sit the student near a good role model

- Break long assignments into smaller parts or shorten the assignments

- Allow extra time to complete assigned work

- Pair written instructions with oral instructions

- Ask the student questions to allow them to participate in the class discussion

- Involve the student in planning the lessons to engage them in their education

- Set up a private signal with the teacher that tells the student to pay attention without embarrassing them

[28] Seay, Bob. (2022, October 28). Accommodations to Include in Your Child's IEP. *ADDitude.* https://www.additudemag.com/20-adhd-accommodations-that-work/.

- Schedule a five-minute meeting before turning in homework or tests to go over their work

- Ignore minor inappropriate behavior

- Increase immediacy of rewards and consequences

- Acknowledge correct answers only when they raise their hand and are called upon

- Send daily or weekly progress reports

- Set up a behavior contract

- Recommend binders with dividers and folders for organization

- Supervise writing down of assignments

- Allow student to keep a set of books at home to help with forgetfulness

- Invite student to run errands if they are acting restless

- Provide short breaks between assignments

- Set up social behavior goals with student and implement rewards

- Encourage cooperative learning tasks

- Assign special responsibilities to social peer groups

- Compliment positive behavior to help build their leadership skills

- Encourage socializing with classmates

- Acknowledge appropriate behavior and good work frequently

- Encourage student to walk away when they are angry

Depending on the severity of your son or daughter's ADHD, it is likely they might not need many accommodations. But, even if they have a long list of accommodations, it is essential to explain to your son or daughter that these things are not punishments. Some of these things will make them feel singled out or embarrassed. From time to time, my daughter hated leaving her classroom to take tests because it made her feel like she did not belong.

It is also essential to understand that these accommodations are not meant to be a cure-all for their ADHD. They cannot erase the behaviors entirely, but they help them build the skills they need to succeed in the classroom. And, even if these modifications do not help, other alternatives exist to traditional education, such as homeschooling, online public schools, charter schools, and focused private schools. Conventional education is not a one-size-fits-all solution. So, if it does not work for your son or daughter, that does not mean they've failed. It simply means that you found one way that did not work.

If that is the case, you keep advocating for them by exploring other options. The world is much more advanced now than it was when we were in school. You will be able to find plenty of opportunities to explore solutions that are a better fit for your daughter or son.

Chapter 5:

Are Your Friends A Good

Influence On You?

Finding a friend group that does not encourage unhealthy habits like vaping or drinking alcohol to resolve conflict is imperative. While always the case with teens, this is also critical for those teens with ADHD who already have extreme trouble navigating or regulating emotions. With my daughter, it only took one introduction to vaping for her to become reliant on it to focus at school or fall asleep at night. She also had friends who introduced her to marijuana and alcohol and a friend who showed her how to self-harm. We have already explored how hazardous those behaviors can be, though we have not quite addressed the power of peer pressure and influence.

My daughter loved and trusted her friends; after all, she went to them for advice when she could not find a way to address the chaos and unpredictability in her life. More often than not, your son or daughter might place their trust in the people they spend most of their time with outside the home. They trust them, and in many cases, they look up to them. So, what reason would they have to discredit their advice?

My daughter was not a victim of peer pressure; she was a victim of peer influence. Whether good or bad, their friends will influence the clothes they wear, how they speak, their activities, and their daily habits. Our hope for our sons and daughters is that their friends are having a good impact on them, but this is not always the case.

Characteristics of a Good Friend

My daughter needed a lot of guidance to navigate through her friend groups, especially when she developed toxic habits that worsened her ADHD symptoms. Every teenager struggles with this because they desperately want to be accepted by their peers, but it gets complicated when someone they care about tries to lead them down a wrong path. Once we highlighted where the problem originated, I opened the pathway to a conversation about what a good, caring friend is like.

Supportive of a Clean and Healthy Lifestyle

Even as adults, we are influenced by the people we spend most of our time with, but it is even harder for teenagers because of their desire to be loved and accepted by a group of friends. So, who they choose to spend most of their time with will heavily influence their choices. That happened to my daughter when her friends talked her into trying drugs, alcohol, vaping, and self-harming.

My daughter has always made her friends a priority in her life, and it was impossible for her to stop a friendship solely because that person would vape, drink alcohol, and/or use pills. She would beg and plead with me to continue to hang out with those friends. She would explain that just because one of her friends vaped or drank alcohol, it didn't mean that friend was a bad person. It was heartbreaking for me to hear her say this, but it is true. My daughter, who relied on those substances, was not a bad person. She was a wonderful person. And I think she was trying to tell me that she was not a bad person despite everything she was going through. It still breaks my heart when I think of this. My daughter would also say she could continue hanging out with her friends, but she just wouldn't vape or drink with them. But, at 12 years old, the reality was that she was not strong enough for this. And she was in too much turmoil and was doing whatever she could to make her feel better. She could not stop vaping. She could not stop drinking. Once she started drinking alcohol, she would not just drink with them but also would drink alone at home in her bedroom. She needed help to stop, and the friends she had were not the ones to help her with this. As parents, we want our kids to do things that make them happy, not things that threaten their health or safety. And I tried my hardest to make my daughter understand that having friends who did not encourage her to experiment with things that could harm her was necessary. I knew that my daughter was in pain, but any drugs or alcohol she drank made this pain worse, not better. And I knew that she wanted to get better. And in fact, she knew that she just didn't want to get better. She needed to get better.

Positive Attitude

It was important to me that my daughter understood that we want people in our lives who look at the world and see hope, faith, and happiness. People who are happy with the way they see the world do not typically experiment with drugs on a whim. They get involved with drugs and alcohol when they feel like they have nothing else to comfort them.

It took a change of environment and meeting new people for my daughter to find friends that were a good example. And once she did, I saw a huge difference in her demeanor. She smiled and joked more. She was happier at home. She was less angry. She was not discouraged and tried new things. And that is what we hope that friends will do for our kids. We want them to have friends who shine a light on their best parts. Finding the right friend group may not happen overnight, but it will happen. And it isn't the number of friends. It could be a tribe of ten or a tribe of two. The amount of positivity and encouragement is what counts, not the number of people it comes from.

Inclusive of Others

One of the things that makes ADHD so challenging is how it makes our children feel like they do not belong. They feel like their disorder singles them out and tells other children their age to stay away from them. This fact comes to light often in school when kids treat them like something is wrong with them. Bullying is still very much a real and present danger among our teenagers today, and there is not always an adult around to do something about it.

Luckily, however, not all the peers your daughter or son will meet will be bullies. In fact, most of them will likely be good influences who invite a diverse selection of their peers into their friend group. Our kids need these types of friend groups because it helps them develop healthy social behavior and models great habits for them as they get older.

Surrounding themselves with an inclusive group of friends will teach them a lot of positive habits:

- It will encourage them to celebrate the fact that everyone is unique.

- It exposes them to different cultures and ways of thinking, opening their minds to new experiences.

- It surrounds them with a group of people who will accept them for who they are, no matter what that entails.

- It encourages curiosity and courage in a world that tries to make everyone the same.

- It instills confidence in them and shows them they are worthy of love and acceptance.

- It gives them a positive reason to be more social and active with their friends.

The first step I took toward helping my daughter identify

which peers might be more inclusive was to show her how to be more accepting of others. First and foremost, our children tend to look up to us, often modeling their lives after what they see us doing. I have strived to show her how important it is to celebrate diversity by celebrating it myself, in the people around me and in her.

Our children are unique individuals who deserve to be celebrated, lifted up, and recognized for the immense gifts they offer the world. Inclusivity is the first step toward showing them how much we value the beautiful young adults they are growing up to be.

Encourages Healthy Extracurricular Activities

At first, my daughter had some challenges finding the right group of friends. I worried she might, through no fault of her own, end up making friends with more friends who might introduce her to unhealthy habits and activities. So, we went through a lot of trial and error to find the right group of friends who could help her turn her social life around into a more positive experience.

One of the things that helped tremendously was getting her involved in some healthy extracurricular activities. As she shed her addictions to alcohol, vaping, and other drugs, we felt that finding an activity she loved would help distract her from returning to those addictions. We started with her school counselor to get a list of extracurricular activities that could have a positive influence on her:

- Subject-related after-school groups (French Club, Debate Club, Science Club, etc.)

- Clubs that would challenge her intellectually (like Chess Club)

- School Sports

- Journalism (newspaper staff or the yearbook)

- Electives that inspire her artistic side (photography, visual art, drama, etc.)

- Girl Scouts

Once we found an activity that would hold her attention, I started to see a positive change in her social life. She made connections with others who loved being a part of the group, and they quickly became close friends and accountability partners who were there to support each other.

It did take us some time to find the right place for her, though. Teenagers with ADHD need activities that engage them at a higher level because it gives them an outlet after school to explore the things they love. They need this because it helps them balance the schoolwork and chores at home that they do not like to do, and it gives them something to look forward to at the end of their school day.

Our kids need a place that belongs to them, and that makes them feel like they belong to something more meaningful than a life full of obligations and challenges. It gives them purpose, and it also helps them look forward to their future as an adult when they get to make their own choices without being bogged down by the expectations their peers and teachers have for them. These extracurricular activities give them a place to explore being happy again.

Navigating Away from Bad Influences

Nobody is perfect, so our kids need to understand that there is room for them to make mistakes and start fresh if they get off on the wrong footing. This is what I worked to instill in my daughter as we coped with her addictions. She needed to know that there was a path away from the chaos that was ripping through her life. So, we started working on a set of cognitive tools she could use should she ever find herself in another group of friends who tried to influence her negatively.

Developing Willpower

As my daughter navigated past her addictions, I knew we had to work on her willpower to walk away from those destructive habits. I stood by her side as she tossed away her vape, made a commitment to get sober, and turned her back on the bad influences. Those were the first hard steps we had to take together to set her up for future success.

After she did that, we took some time together to list everything she wanted to achieve in the future. This list covered short-term goals (doing better in school) and long-term goals (plans for her career after graduation), and we listed the steps she needed to take to accomplish these achievements. Not only did this help build her willpower, but it also helped reignite her focus on her future.

Beyond that, making this list also gave her something to look at whenever she felt inclined to return to her addictions or the friends who encouraged those toxic habits. Rather than simply telling herself she couldn't vape or drink alcohol, it gave her options for what she *could* do that would help her become the amazing young woman she wanted to be.

Here is the hard truth: Our kids hate being told what to do.

Even as adults, they tend to do the exact opposite of what we advise them to do. But, when they have a choice between several alternatives, they are well-equipped to make the right decision that ensures their happiness, safety, and health. Being able to make these choices for themselves helps build their confidence and sense of self-worth, which is something that can feel pretty challenging for a teenager with ADHD.

Defining Healthy Habits

On that list we created together, I also helped my daughter develop several healthy habits she could practice instead of engaging in her addictions. These are some of the healthy alternatives we explored:

- Drawing, writing, photography, or some other artistic pursuit that engaged her mind

- Playing chess, cards, or board games with friends or family members

- Reading on a subject that interested her

- Going online (or to the library) to research career options for her future

- Taking a family trip to the zoo, museum, art gallery,

the movies, or a convention that sounded fun

- Walking around the block, doing yoga, lifting weights, or dancing to boost her endorphins

- Watching a funny movie or television show

- Writing her feelings down in a journal, then talking about them together

- Doing fun chores around the house together or on her own

- Working on homework together

- Calling a friend to hang out

- Learning something new that interested her

- Going shopping for a new outfit, game, or book to reward her continued sobriety

This activity gave her a list of infinite possibilities she could turn to in order to distract her from wanting to vape, drink, use drugs, or isolate herself. It has been a really great tool for her to use, and I am proud of the hard work she has done to continue choosing healthy alternatives to her addictions.

Finding Treatment for Addiction

If your son or daughter fell into an addiction like mine, I want you to know that you are not alone. And you shouldn't feel like you have to navigate this alone, either. There is help out there for both of you, and I strongly encourage you to explore all your options for recovery.

However you decide to handle your son or daughter's addiction is a personal choice that your family will have to make together, and nobody can tell you what that path should look like. With that in mind, though, I highly encourage you to seek out the advice of an addiction professional as you explore your options; even better if this professional has experience working with addicts with ADHD.

Helping your teenager with ADHD through an addiction holds its own set of problems. Once my daughter got into the habit of using these substances to self-soothe, she could not stop. Thus, she had to be treated for addiction before she was treated for her ADHD, so the medical professionals could determine what exactly was causing, specifically, her mood swings, depression, and anger. Was she angry because she was in withdrawal or frustrated with her

ADHD symptoms? It was a very scary time for us because it created a dangerous circle that still left my daughter feeling frustrated, overwhelmed, and lost in the face of her symptoms.

As you get through this together, you will have many wins and losses. Addiction is a hard habit to walk away from because those toxic substances try their hardest to stick around. They will be tempted several times every day in the beginning because the urge to abuse those substances does not simply go away when they choose to stop. There are other hard lessons you might need to learn along the way. Safe Landing, a recovery organization for teens, has several reminders for you as you travel this path:[29]

1. It is not your fault as a parent that your teen got addicted.

2. It is also not the fault of your son or daughter.

3. Enabling your teenager can make things worse.

4. Harsh punishment will not help your child stay clean,

---

[29] 13 Things to Understand About Teen Substance Abuse. (n.d.). Safe Landing. Accessed on March 3, 2023, from https://www.safelanding recovery.com/blog/13-things-parents-dont-get-about-teen-substance-abuse/.

either.

5. Pain lies at the root of addiction.

6. Your child has to choose recovery if you decide to enroll them in a treatment program.

7. They will need a lot of support while trying to stay sober.

8. Sobriety does not happen overnight; it takes time.

9. They might say things they do not mean as they struggle in recovery.

10. It only takes a brief moment to slip back into their addiction.

11. Your teen's relapse does not mean they are a failure.

12. You cannot do everything for them.

13. Parents need to take care of themselves too.

I had to remind myself of many of these things as I helped my daughter recover. It was not easy, but it was worth it in the end because she found her way out of her addiction, and that missing light returned to her life. You and your teen will get through this, too, and then you can focus on helping them manage the ADHD symptoms that led them to their addiction in the first place.

Chapter 6:

How Can I Help You Find Treatment?

Treating ADHD is not an easy fix, and your situation is unique. Some teens find medications helpful, while others choose to follow a life-management plan and determine what works best for them. No matter how you decide to treat your son or daughter's ADHD, you will find the right conditions to help your child regain their focus, regulate their emotions, and navigate through their impaired executive functioning. We found what works best for us by exploring the options available through four treatment categories.

Behavioral Therapy

Behavioral therapy is always a great place to start when dealing with improving mental health. It gives both you and your teen a voice and a chance to explore all the treatment options available that your psychologist and/or psychiatrist recommend. Keeping regular appointments with both types of mental health professionals will set your daughter or son up with a highly skilled professional support team that works together to come up with a treatment plan to improve the bigger picture — the ultimate happiness and success you want to see your child return to for a better future.

Therapy (Psychologist)

There is not one tried-and-true method that will solve all your problems. Treatment for ADHD is complicated, but it needs to start somewhere. Starting your journey through therapy with a psychologist specializing in ADHD will put you on the right path to relieving your teen's ADHD symptoms. Many therapists cannot prescribe medication if they feel it will help, but they can recommend that your teen see a psychiatrist.

Beyond that, however, psychologists do have a lot of cognitive tools in their arsenal that will set your child up with coping techniques, training for you as a parent, and activities that will set a positive foundation for their whole treatment journey.

If your child has a comorbidity with other mental health concerns, your therapist will have recommendations for cognitive therapy methods. However, if you only have an ADHD diagnosis, those types of treatments will be ineffective in improving your son or daughter's outlook on their mental health. For this reason, many behavioral treatments your psychologist will recommend will focus on strategies for you and your child to help improve your daily lives.

Therapy (Psychiatrist)

While most psychologists cannot give you an official diagnosis, psychiatrists can because they are medical doctors with the training and licensure to diagnose and prescribe medication to treat those disorders. Pediatricians also serve this function well, especially those specializing in ADHD and other developmental disorders. However, pediatricians are not normally trained in therapy protocols.

The psychiatrist's first role is to dive deep and discover what is happening with your daughter or son. At first, they will interview you and your teen to identify behaviors and symptoms you feel point to a potential ADHD diagnosis. They will take a complete cognitive and emotional background to get an overview of any challenges affecting your child's success.

At our first appointment, our psychiatrist spent about an hour simply listening to our challenges at home and school to determine what could be happening in my daughter's life. I found it extremely helpful to walk into this appointment with my daughter's symptoms written down so we did not leave anything out that could help us get an accurate diagnosis. It can also be of great value to write down some questions to ask if you have any lingering concerns about your child's mental well-being.

Sometimes this initial interview is enough for your psychiatrist to diagnose, but it is not a perfect system. Doctors can make mistakes; after all, they are only human, just like us. The mental health industry has come a long way in identifying the symptoms and causes of various mental health challenges, but researchers are constantly learning new things about ADHD.

For instance, though ADHD is one of the most common diagnoses among children experiencing developmental issues, it is also one of the most misdiagnosed disorders, according to the *Pre-Collegiate Global Health Review (PGHR)*.[30]

---

[30] The Global Misdiagnosis of ADHD and the Devastating Long-Term Effects. (2021, August 11). *Pre-Collegiate Global Health Review.*

This is why psychologists and psychiatrists care to ensure your son or daughter gets the right diagnosis.

Journaling

It might sound simple, but journaling is a great therapy tool allowing your teen to express all their emotions without judgment. This tool helps prevent those unregulated emotions from erupting and manifesting unpredictably. It will also help give your child more confidence in expressing their thoughts and ideas, which is an area that typically needs a bit of work when dealing with a teenager with ADHD.

Beyond the benefits you see at home and in school, a journal also gives your daughter or son's support team access to their daily struggles, which can be incredibly effective in getting the proper diagnosis. This technique works well because your teen might not know how to communicate the inner workings of their mind easily. But, with a filled-out journal in hand, your therapist can refer to certain entries to get a better picture of what is going on with your child.

These journals can either be an open-minded flow of their

https://www.pghr.org/post/the-global-misdiagnosis-of-adhd-and-the-devastating-long-term-effects.

thoughts, or their therapist might give them specific prompts to write about or questions to answer in their journal. Amy Launder, a licensed therapist, offers some helpful examples of therapeutic writing prompts to help get into the habit of therapeutic journaling:[31]

- If you could go anywhere in the world right now, where would you be, and why?

- Is there anyone with whom you feel you can be your full self unapologetically? Who is this person, and what about them makes you feel so free?

- Is there a dream or a nightmare that you have over and over again? Without looking it up, what do you personally think it means?

- What is the thing you fear the most in the world? Do you think this fear is valid? What does it stop you from doing? What would you do differently if you didn't have this fear?

- Have you cried happy tears? What made it happen? Why do you think it affected you that way?

---

[31] Launder, Amy. (2020, April 30). 20 Therapeutic Journal Prompts. https://www.amylaunder.com/blog/20-therapeutic-journal-prompts.

- Is there a song lyric that really motivates you and helps you push through difficult times? What's the lyric? How does it inspire you?

- Is there a lie you've told recently that you regret? Why did you tell it? Who did you lie to? What would have happened if you had told the truth?

- What have you said yes to recently that you wished you had said no to? What stopped you from saying no?

- What does unconditional love mean to you?

- Who do you admire the most in the world and why?

Most journaling prompts are not designed to elicit a specific, predictable response. They are meant to get your teen to communicate positively about their feelings. Even if your therapist does not use this as a tool, you can use these types of journaling prompts to open a line of communication with your son or daughter. You might learn something new about them!

Psychosocial Treatments

Behavioral therapy is extremely important to get your teen on the right path, especially if you do not have a diagnosis for them yet. However, it will not cure your son or daughter's ADHD symptoms. Easing those symptoms is an ongoing process that involves psychosocial treatment to regulate thought patterns, behavioral challenges, and emotional intelligence. There are many methodologies to help with this, but I will talk briefly about the three that have helped my daughter tremendously.

Problem-Solving Skills

Because her executive functioning skills were underdeveloped, my daughter had a lot of challenges when she tried to solve her own problems. She was ill-equipped to come up with possible solutions that might help her ADHD symptoms, ultimately leading to her adopting some toxic behaviors. Once we treated her addictions, we started working on building up those problem-solving skills so she could find some relief from her frustrations without resorting to dangerous self-soothing activities.

Problem-solving at an intellectual level involves eight separate steps. We often go through these internally without thinking about the different steps we took to solve a problem. The University of Iowa breaks this down into eight actionable steps, and I have added my thoughts about how we can help our teens with ADHD through this process:[32]

1. **Define the problem.**

   Communicating their problems clearly is an issue for teenagers with ADHD. So, sometimes we need to ask them specific questions to investigate what lies at the heart of the problem. You can start by asking your daughter or son, "What happened that upset you?" Then, from there, you can talk about the entire problem, how it started, how it made them feel, and why they think they need to resolve it. Once you have the problem adequately defined, the rest gets much easier.

2. **Clarify the problem.**

   If you are unclear on some details, you can ask your child questions that allow them to speak more specifically about the problem. You want to move

---

[32] 8-Step Problem-Solving Process. (n.d.) University of Iowa. Accessed March 4, 2023, from https://hr.uiowa.edu/development/organizational-development/lean/8-step-problem-solving-process.

beyond the general problem and talk about the events that led up to the problem. For instance, if it involves declining grades in school, you can ask about the class they are having issues with, how they found out about the failing grade, what their everyday challenges are in the class, etc.

3. **Define the goal.**

Next, it is helpful to talk about what result they would like to see. In our school example, you can ask your teen to get specific about what grade they are aiming for in their class. Note: it does not have to be an A! This step allows them to measure when they are done solving the problem, and it will help them tremendously to see that there is an actual end to their challenges.

4. **Identify the root cause of the problem.**

This step is especially helpful if they have to deal with this problem regularly. In our school example, maybe they are getting behind in their schoolwork weekly. A problem like that might require a deeper dive to understand why they feel so challenged by their classes.

5. **Develop an action plan.**

This is where you will help your son or daughter work on their executive functioning skills. Here, you will come up with a list of possible solutions together by asking them more questions; then, you can discuss which option sounds like the best solution. You will list all the minor and major steps they need to take, leaving nothing out. Since ADHD teenagers have challenges with step-by-step processes, having it all written out will help them follow through with the plan.

6. **Execute action plan.**

Next, they will tackle the solution one small step at a time. In the beginning, they might feel overwhelmed if it requires a lot of steps, but that is okay. This process will take a lot of practice to get used to. You can have them mark off each step as they finish so they know how much further they have to go.

7. **Evaluate the results.**

You can sit together and go over what went right and wrong throughout the problem-solving process. Give them a safe space to talk about what was the most

125

challenging part, and you can earmark that to work on closely the next time you solve a problem together. As you are evaluating the results, you can ask them why they thought it worked or why they thought it did not work. This will also help develop their critical thinking skills.

8. **Continuously improve.**

If the problem you solved rears its ugly head regularly, then that gives your daughter or son plenty of room to work on how they will solve it in the future. This is especially helpful for homework or chores they do around the house because these things will continue to challenge them.

I know this sounds like a lot to a teenager with ADHD, but it does not have to all be tackled in one day. Take it one step at a time, especially in the beginning when they are getting used to this problem-solving process. Over time, it will get much easier for them, and you might eventually find that they develop the habit of doing this independently.

Methods for Managing Behavior

"Behavior Management" is a term mental health professionals use that describes the training and education parents of ADHD children should have to help them manage their ADHD symptoms. CHADD recommends focusing on five pillars that help you manage your teenager's symptoms, and I have added my thoughts about each of these behavior management techniques:[33]

- **Start with goals the child can achieve in small steps.**

  Because it can take some time for your son or daughter to get used to a different way of doing things, they need to start out small. If you are teaching them how to do laundry, for example, you can have them start the process until they get used to it. As they feel more comfortable, you can add steps that cover the entire process of finishing one load of laundry.

- **Be consistent across different times of the day, different settings, and different people.**

  Your teenager needs consistency to build up their executive functioning skills. If you only implement

---

[33] ADHD Quick Facts: Behavior Management in ADHD Treatment. (n.d.). CHADD. Accessed March 4, 2023, from https://chadd.org/about-adhd/adhd-quick-facts-behavior-management-in-adhd-treatment/.

specific guidelines for them at home, then their life can potentially suffer in other areas. This is especially important when dealing with multiple adults supervising your daughter or son in the house, like another parent, grandparent, or older sibling. Everyone must hold their teenager accountable.

- **Provide consequences immediately following behavior.**

One thing that worked well for us was creating a behavior contract. I outlined what behavior was unacceptable and the consequences my daughter would face if she displayed these behaviors. After that, I had to stick to my guns and consistently implement those consequences. My daughter needed that stability to reinforce what was expected of her.

- **Implement behavioral interventions over the long haul, not just for a few months.**

To further develop your consistency, you must ensure these guidelines are in place for the long term. This will help them build consistent patterns in their life that live well into their adult years, setting them up for future success and happiness.

- **Teaching and learning new skills takes time. The child's improvement will be gradual. Enjoy each step.**

- With an ADHD teenager, patience is definitely a virtue! Through no fault of their own, they will need gentle reminders of what they need to do throughout the day at home, in school, and at work, if they have an after-school job. It may take some time, but they *will* improve on their own timeline.

ADHD Training for Teachers

Just like parents need the training to work with ADHD teenagers, some teachers need additional training to understand the social, cognitive, and behavioral challenges that exist when educating students with ADHD symptoms. Our sons and daughters spend nearly 1,000 hours with them every school year, so they need to be prepared for the challenges ahead. The training available for both parents and teachers typically employs a Pavlovian methodology, where positive (or expected) behavior is rewarded, and unacceptable behaviors are met with consequences.[34]

---

[34] van der Oord, S., & Tripp, G. (2020). How to Improve Behavioral Parent and Teacher Training for Children with ADHD: Integrating

These methodologies work well for many teenagers with ADHD when they are exposed to these rewards and consequences in both settings, which is one of the pillars we discussed earlier in this chapter. When these techniques are reinforced consistently, your son or daughter can better work through their impaired executive functioning.

Medication

When my daughter's doctor first recommended medication for her ADHD, I had my concerns about the effects the stimulants might have on her brain long-term, especially considering she had already struggled with her addiction to substances. Since these medications had many of the same effects on the brain as some illegal stimulants widely used by addicts, the thought of introducing this medication to my daughter stressed me out. But, as I researched, I learned more about ADHD brain chemistry and felt comfortable including it in her treatment.

Empirical Research on Learning and Motivation into Treatment. *Clinical child and family psychology review*, 23(4), 577–604. https://doi.org/10.1007/s10567-020-00327-z.

Medication + Behavioral Therapy

Medication alone, however, did not equip my daughter with the tools she needed to be happy and successful. These pharmaceuticals are not intended as a cure, though they help the brain accomplish the tasks they need throughout the day.

Though stimulants had been prescribed regularly before their publication, the APA published a study in 2001 that talked about the contradictory effects prescribed stimulants had on adolescents with ADHD over their neurotypical peers. Conducted by a team at the University of Pittsburgh, researchers found that these medications — along with other behavioral therapy — not only allowed students to complete their work but also with more accuracy. They also noted it "improved students' performance on a range of academic measures, including note-taking, daily assignments, and quiz scores, without causing major side effects."[35]

Today, this is the standard for treating many teenagers with ADHD when their symptoms prevent them from paying

---

[35] Carpenter, Siri. (2001, May). Stimulants boost achievement in ADHD teens. *Monitor* *on* *Psychology.* https://www.apa.org/monitor/may01/stimulants.

attention, following directions, or exhibiting self-control in the classroom. It has worked well for my daughter and many other teenagers whose lives have been disrupted by this disorder.

Solving the Addiction Problem

Oddly enough, ADHD medications also can prevent addiction in teenagers with this disorder, according to a study published in *The Journal of Child Psychology and Psychiatry*. The medical research study indicated that the addiction rate among prescribed stimulants for ADHD dropped 31% in 2009, illustrating a drastic reduction in documented cases of addiction. They also found that the longer a patient takes the medication, the more preventative it is.[36]

However, these results will be much different if the medication is not taken as prescribed by your child's doctor. So, you and your teen must explicitly follow your psychiatrist's instructions to prevent addiction and ensure

---

[36] Chang, Z., Lichtenstein, P., Halldner, L., D'Onofrio, B., Serlachius, E., Fazel, S., Långström, N., & Larsson, H. (2013). Stimulant ADHD medication and risk for substance abuse. *Journal of Child Psychology and Psychiatry, 55*(8), 878–885. https://doi.org/10.1111/jcpp.12164.

the best long-term effects for their treatment.

Structured Activities

Structure is extremely important for adolescents with ADHD because they will have other areas in their lives that feel out of control. Combine that unpredictability with their impaired self-control, and they are left feeling overwhelmed, a little lost, and without purpose. Structured activities — such as school sports, after-school clubs, drama, and debate — can help counteract these negative side effects of ADHD.

In school, my daughter often felt like she was not good enough because of how challenging many of her classes were, especially with a heavy load of homework to complete every weekend. However, when she got involved with various extracurricular activities, she found outlets that helped her build her confidence the more she participated in these activities.

We noticed the following other improvements in her life:

1. After-school play and sports gave her an outlet to work off her excess energy.

2. School became more interesting because the extracurricular activities engaged her mind in ways that she controlled.

3. She made great friends who had a positive influence on her.

4. The sense of achievement inspired her to find other ways to reach goals in school.

5. The activities gave her something to look forward to and improved her mood, helping her regulate her emotions more.

These activities alone, however, were not enough to see an overall improvement in her brain function. A one-dimensional treatment plan might benefit your child, but we saw a much bigger positive effect once we combined all these treatment methodologies. The changes will not appear overnight, but you will see them if you are consistent and patient with your son or daughter.

Chapter 7:

Can I Talk to You About ADHD?

Teens with ADHD do want help. Desperately. My daughter would beg for therapy. When my teenager tried vaping or drinking alcohol to help her restlessness and calm the thoughts in her head, those things were not hidden well in her room. She was not shy in saying that she needed help, but she didn't know what to ask for. The way she tried to show me she needed help was often detrimental to her health, triggering a need for a better way to communicate.

When we started weighing our options to find the best therapy for her, I initiated a four-step process to ensure the best possible outcome.

Step One: Research Online to Find the Right Psychologists and Psychiatrists

Before digging into online lists of local mental health

providers, I created a system that would help me evaluate the available options. I knew these criteria for the person who would ultimately help my daughter would need to extend beyond impressive credentials. While that is important, I knew we needed a level of trust and commitment that those credentials could not provide.

Experience with ADHD

At the top of my list, I knew our priority had to be extensive experience with teenagers diagnosed with ADHD. Beyond that, I also thought it would be a bonus if they had experience with late-onset ADHD because my daughter was a bit older than the diagnostic criteria provided. This priority has been critical to my daughter's success because I realize now that not all psychologists and psychiatrists have the same expertise as their peers. With that as one of my deciding factors, I came up with a list of questions I could ask before we decided on the right person to help us.

Experience with Teenagers

Teenagers with ADHD have a different set of challenges than adults or younger children. One of the reasons for this is that children under the age of twelve have a much different set of responsibilities than teenagers. I expected more of my daughter at fourteen than I did at five years old, which revealed many challenges her impaired executive functioning brought on.

I knew that if I could find someone more experienced with teenagers, they would understand exactly what we were dealing with in our everyday life. More than anything, my daughter needed that connection if she was ever going to return to that happy girl from the video.

A Certain Level of Empathy

Not every mental health professional starts their career for altruistic reasons, and that has the potential to bring mixed results to patients. So, once I started my search online, I began to look at publicly posted reviews to get a feel for how they made their patients feel. Beyond connection, my daughter also needed some understanding and patience to overcome these challenging ADHD symptoms.

We had dealt with uncaring medical professionals in the past, and it left us feeling lost and alone when the gatekeepers to the help we needed did not make an effort to care about our situation. With my daughter having her own communication challenges, I had to advocate for her in this regard, so I would not budge on finding the right person to help.

Proven Results with Patients

None of the above criteria means much of anything if the psychologist or psychiatrist is incapable of helping your child. Though this is not always easy information to find, I wanted to talk with some available therapists at least to learn about their methodologies and how those techniques have helped their patients.

Then, after I developed this system of evaluating mental health professionals, I took a deep dive online to find professionals who were accepting new patients. Obviously, if you have insurance limitations, you will need to consider that in your search. But, if you can extend your search beyond that, you will have many more options when you make your final decision.

Step Two: Make Sure Your Child is Comfortable

Though I did not mention it above, one last thing is essential when searching for the right mental health provider — giving your son or daughter autonomy over their care. For them to get the help they deserve, they need to feel like they have control over who they see.

Throughout their treatment, they will spend many hours with this person, talking about their challenges, obstacles, stressors, and roadblocks, and they will also be talking about their hopes and dreams for their future. I wanted to give my daughter the freedom to be open and honest with her therapist, so more than anything, she had to be comfortable with this person.

Before we started talking to potential psychologists and psychiatrists, I sat down and had a heart-to-heart with her to determine what *she* was looking for in a therapist. As we have already discussed, I had my own criteria to consider, but listening to her feelings was also critical to this process.

These are some of the things she felt would be important in a therapist:

- I want to believe I can tell them anything without judgment.

  Having a therapist who can set their personal feelings aside for their patients is extremely important to kids, especially teenagers, who might have questionable thoughts or experiences they need to work through. Even as an adult, opening yourself up to potential judgment is difficult and even harder for adolescents. Because if they feel their therapist will judge them for something they say or do, they will likely not feel comfortable with them in the long-term. If your son or daughter is going to find any relief from talking to a new person about their thoughts, feelings, and ideas, they need to be able to express themselves in a stress-free environment.

- My therapist should be a great listener.

  One of the most important things to find in a therapist is someone who will listen. This type of listening goes much deeper than simply hearing what the other person is saying. My daughter wanted someone who would listen and consider what she said as important as she did. A therapist who listens might take notes, ask questions to verify or dive deeper or come back to things your teenager has said in other sessions (or earlier in the current one). If their therapist cannot listen well enough, you might run the risk of getting a misdiagnosis or a treatment plan that does not work as well as it should.

- I need to be able to trust that they care about helping

me.

Too often, mental health professionals give excuses when listening to patients' concerns because they have likely heard it all before. But, for your teenager to be really comfortable with their therapist, they need to know they are taken seriously. They do not want to be placed in the same box as another patient who has different challenges, symptoms, and issues than your child does. When this happens, you hear statements like, "That is normal," or "That is not a concern." Teenagers do not bring things up in a therapy session if it does not concern them, and they need to know their therapist takes their concerns seriously.

- They should give me some great techniques for doing better in school.

School is a major concern for teenagers with ADHD because they have to work extremely hard to focus in class, pay attention to their teachers, and get their homework done at home every day. Especially if their ADHD diagnosis is recent, they might feel lost and confused when doing schoolwork. It is a huge stressor for them that they hope a mental health professional can help them with. Of course, they can get more focused help from their teachers and counselors, but as their therapist gets to know them on a deeper level, they might have some insights that could help them further to give them some peace of mind.

- My therapist should understand that talking about hard things does not feel good.

One of my daughter's ADHD symptoms was a lack of communication skills, so opening up to a new therapist was not an easy task. Even though she believed her therapist would not judge her, it was still hard and challenging for her to bring up the more intricate subjects, like her past drinking, vaping, and alcohol issues. She needed a therapist who would show her kindness, empathy, and understanding in the face of the topics she was afraid to share.

Step Three: Commit to Going to Therapy Regularly

Going to see a psychologist or psychiatrist is not the same as going to the doctor when you have the flu. ADHD will not simply go away with a pill or a few months of treatment. Unfortunately, this is a disorder your daughter or son will struggle with throughout the rest of their life. They might not always be as symptomatic as they are now, but they will still need to seek ongoing treatment, medication, and/or a combination of the two for an extended period.

Another essential thing to remember is that seeing great results from therapy takes time. It is an ongoing effort that requires everyone involved to be committed to the results they want to see. You will need to make a commitment to your child to facilitate their therapy appointments and treatment modalities, and they will need to make a commitment to themselves to continue working on improving their symptoms.

In the beginning, this commitment might mean that your teen needs to attend therapy appointments once a week. This frequency might feel overwhelming, especially if they have difficulty opening up to their therapist. If this is the case, it is helpful to remind them that it will get easier as they attend more therapy sessions.

If it takes your daughter or son some time to adjust, there are many ways you can support them through this journey:[37]

- Be available for your teen if they need to talk about their therapy sessions.

  My daughter did not always want to talk about her sessions afterward, but I made sure to let her know that we could talk if she wanted. I knew that if I pressured her to talk about the therapy sessions, she might not be as open to communicating with me in the future. Keeping that line of communication open is extremely important to the success of their treatment because those sessions depend on your son or daughter understanding they have a choice and the freedom to say what they need to without any pressure.

---

[37] How To Support Your Teen Through Therapy. (n.d.). Ashley Therapy. Accessed on March 6, 2023, from https://www.ashleytreatment.org/rehab-blog/support-teens-therapy/.

- Encourage positive self-talk when they speak unkindly about themselves.

Thinking and speaking negatively about herself was a hard habit for my daughter to break, so I knew it would take some time. Being kind about this challenge helped her tremendously in her treatment because she did not feel as though I judged her for the things she said. She needed understanding and encouragement, not forceful correction. We also had helpful conversations about why she felt that way about herself. She loved being able to speak freely about these negative thoughts without getting in trouble for them.

- Support and encourage them as they complete the assignments their therapist gives them.

As her therapy progressed, my daughter's therapist gave her easy assignments to do at home that would complement her treatment. She gave her things like daily breathing exercises, conversation starters, journal entry prompts, and coping techniques she could use daily when she felt challenged by a specific task. I allowed her to do them independently but encouraged and supported her when needed. I am proud of all her work in her treatment, and I knew this encouragement would make it easier for her to continue.

- Understand that they might want some privacy about the specific things they discussed with their therapist.

It was sometimes hard for my daughter to open up to her therapist about certain things. I knew she would have to talk about some hard topics, and I did not want to interfere with her confidence to do so. I clarified that I was there to support her therapy but would not pressure her to tell me what she told her therapist. Sometimes she confided in me about her session, and I was happy to listen. However, I did not get my feelings hurt if she did not want to share.

- Check-in with them periodically to see how their therapy is going.

Though you do not need to know everything about your son or daughter's sessions, it is essential to check in occasionally to ensure it is going well. This ensures the line of communication stays open if they grow uncomfortable with their therapist, and it helps support them in whatever they need to keep the momentum going forward. I set aside a time every month to check in with my daughter to talk about all her wins and challenges that she experienced with her therapy that month. However, I also made it clear that she could come to me with any questions or problems she was having along the way.

- Be willing to participate genuinely when your participation is requested in therapy sessions.

In the beginning, I came to a few sessions with my daughter to make sure she was comfortable with her therapist, but I knew there would come a time she would attend these on her own. From time to time, though, the therapist invited me to participate in sessions when they thought my input and insight could be helpful to my daughter's therapy. During those sessions, I came prepared to be honest, understanding, and willing to discuss hard topics if necessary.

Step Four: Follow Through with the Treatment Plan

Setting up a treatment plan will not work if you do not

follow through with it. Participating in the plan requires consistency, patience, understanding, and persistence. This might require you to check in with your child and their therapist to ensure everyone is on the same page. I did check-ins for my daughter not to micromanage the process but to ensure she had all the information she needed to follow through with her treatment plan. Whether simple and straightforward or complex and lengthy, complete dedication is necessary to ensure your daughter or son gets the best care possible.

Once we had a solid treatment plan in place, I made sure I had it all written down, so we did not forget anything her therapist wanted us to do. If it helps, you can put together a folder that lists all the details, including medication schedules, along with important information about the drug; upcoming appointments; behavioral contracts made with the therapist, teachers, and you and your child; coping techniques from counselors and therapists; phone numbers for teachers and doctors; daily exercises from your child's therapist; and any other behavioral treatments recommended.

After each appointment, we sat together to update it if necessary. This step was important because treatment plans tend to evolve for various reasons. For instance, if one of the therapist's recommendations made my daughter feel uncomfortable, we would replace it with something different or remove it entirely. Their comfort is always of the utmost importance, as you will experience many ebbs and flows in how they feel about their treatment plan.

This was one of the reasons why checking in regularly with my daughter about her therapy was so important. Just because she was comfortable in the beginning did not mean she always would be. Even if she could not come out and say, "I'm uncomfortable with this," I could see red flags raised if things ever changed drastically.

Of course, another aspect we have not discussed is your level of comfort with the treatment plan. You also need to feel like you have a voice in your child's treatment because their well-being is always in your hands. If something does not feel right, it is likely your teen also senses something is off. They either might be afraid to raise their voice or not know how to communicate their discomfort.

This treatment plan is not set in stone; you can change it as often as needed. For this process to work for your child, they need to feel comfortable with it. So, anything that causes them anxiety or makes them feel uneasy will either slow their progress or stop it entirely. Continuing along a rocky path nobody wants to be on can undo all the great things that have happened up until that point. So, always remember that you both have a voice and need to use it at all times, especially if something does not feel right.

I have had to advocate many times for my daughter, and I am glad I took the risk and stood up for her rights. You will have moments like this, too, and I know you have the strength to do what is right.

Chapter 8:

What Will Your Future Hold?

When it comes to this disease, there is no guarantee that all the traditional treatment methods will work for your son or daughter. Every teenager with ADHD has symptoms that manifest differently in their individual lives, and those plans need to meet their specific needs and lifestyles. With ADHD being one of the most widely diagnosed childhood developmental disorders in the United States, this also means that there is always research going into new methods for treatment. When I found this out, I was absolutely thrilled because I knew it meant a more promising future for my daughter. After all, their ADHD will be with them for the rest of their lives, and these new treatments will significantly help treat those future issues.

Medications

Just like behavioral treatments do not offer a one-size-fits-all solution, neither do medications. As with all medicine, side effects, if present, will vary from patient to patient, and each patient is unique. It also takes some time to evaluate the effectiveness.

One type of medication used to treat ADHD is prescription stimulants. For some ADHD patients, stimulants work by increasing the levels of the brain chemicals that are often a result of pleasant, calming activities. In addition, stimulant drugs can help a patient focus and remain alert. A patient may report being able to stay on task and organize daily tasks without feeling overwhelmed. There is a new clarity.

Furthermore, there are also prescription medications used to treat ADHD that are non-stimulants. Child Mind Institute writes about reasons you might have for pursuing non-stimulant vs. stimulant ADHD medications:[38]

- Stimulant medications didn't work.

  Stimulant medications can relieve *some* teenagers with ADHD, but these prescriptions are not

---

[38] Miller, Caroline. (2023, January 26). What Are Nonstimulant Medications for ADHD? Child Mind Institute. https://childmind.org/article/what-are-nonstimulant-medications-for-adhd/.

guaranteed. Every child's brain chemistry is different so they will react differently to the stimulants in these medications. For some teenagers, the side effects of the stimulants are too powerful to continue using them. Then, on the other end of the spectrum, some teenagers might not notice any difference at all when they take it as prescribed. This does not mean there is anything wrong with them. It simply means you have found one way that does not work. So, you keep trying until your doctor lands on a combination that works for your daughter or son.

- A child with ADHD might have another disorder as well.

It is pretty common for teenagers with ADHD to have other disorders. For instance, my daughter also had to deal with depression, anxiety, and substance abuse. When managing other disorders on top of the ADHD, the brain's reaction to the stimulants can possibly either have no effect on the patient or have a negative effect on them. For instance, for some patients, these stimulants can have the same effect on the brain as cocaine or methamphetamines might. We get told repeatedly as parents that stimulants are supposed to have the opposite effect on our teen's brains because they have ADHD, but that is not always the case.

- A child can benefit by adding a non-stimulant medication.

As your teenager gets older, you might notice a need to increase the dosage of their stimulant medication. But what happens if that dosage is too high? In cases like this, doctors find that combining the stimulant drug with the non-stimulant one can be extremely helpful in their treatment. This is especially important to consider if you are starting to see some alarming negative side effects from a recent dosage increase. If you have some concerns about those side effects, never be afraid to ask about other options for them. There are several non-stimulant medications out there you can try to see if one works better. (Strattera, Qelbree, Catapres, Kapvay, Tenex, and Intuniv are a few examples of non-stimulant medications you can ask the doctor about.)

- Stimulants could be risky for teenagers with substance-use problems or a history of drug use.

If your child has had substance-abuse issues, these non-stimulant medications would be a great option to look into because they are not supposed to have any addictive ingredients.

Hyperactivity to Improve Working Memory

I know it might seem odd to see a symptom of ADHD listed here as a way to treat the disorder. However, when it is purposeful, it can be quite beneficial for adolescents with ADHD who have issues with their short-term memory, a common symptom of the disorder.

Also known as working memory, it is the part of the brain responsible for holding temporary bits of information that can be useful in doing homework, household chores, and other everyday activities. These are the skills we used as kids to play the memory games where we had to flip over cards and pair the two like images together. This type of activity can be challenging for kids with ADHD because they often have impaired working memory. For instance, when I asked my daughter what she did in school that day, she really meant it when she said she could not remember.

Working memory has three parts: the central executive, the

phonological loop, and the visuospatial sketchpad.[39] In a nutshell, the central executive part of working memory focuses attention, controls the flow of information, and links working memory to long-term memory. The phonological loop takes in the information you hear, and visual information is stored in the visuospatial sketchpad. The sketchpad and the phonological loop work separately, so you can increase your memory by improving both. For example, you may remember a phone number better if you write it down and say it aloud.

When you put these three areas together, the working memory is responsible for the daily tasks your teenager must accomplish:[40]

- Paying attention

  Your teen's attention likely wanes with subjects or activities their brains do not find engaging. This often presents the most challenges in school in classes they struggle with because of how complex the subject is

---

[39] How ADHD Contributes to Memory Problems. (n.d.). THINK Neurology for Kids. Accessed on March 8, 2023, from https://www.thinkkids.com/blog/how-adhd-contributes-to-memory-problems.

[40] Ibid.

for them to understand. This lack of focus can cause them to forget what they should be doing, leading to poor academic performance over time.

- Following instructions

With impaired working memory, teenagers with ADHD have many challenges following instructions. It requires them to remember the order of the steps they have to complete to achieve a goal or finish their chores at home. You have likely had to remind them repeatedly either how to do these tasks or that it is their responsibility to do them in the first place.

- Planning actions

Planning requires a deep understanding of how to accomplish a task from point A to point B, which we have already discussed in length, poses challenges for teenagers with ADHD. Not understanding how to properly plan their day or a homework assignment can feel extremely frustrating, often leading them to ignore it entirely.

- Organizing activities

When my daughter would lose her focus on

organizing something, she would throw it all together in the end, ultimately making it harder for her to find something she needed. On top of that, her poor working memory function meant she would easily forget where she put those things. It created a vicious circle, and she rarely knew where things were when she needed them the most.

- Reaching a goal

Accomplishing a long-term or short-term goal requires a fair amount of planning, which is often challenging for teenagers with ADHD because of their impaired executive functioning. However, our children's daily lives are full of goals they need to achieve both at home and school. They need techniques that can help them develop this part of their brain.

- Scheduling time

Time blindness is a very real thing for our kids who are diagnosed with ADHD. This essentially means they do not know how long a task is going to take, so they are either perpetually late or early to all their appointments or classes. My daughter would always arrive early to her classes so she had time she could control before she had to find her focus when the bell rang. This can also affect our children by not understanding how long it will take to complete a homework assignment, so they often end up turning it in late because they did not plan their time well.

- Staying on track

My daughter got off track easily when doing homework or chores because there was always something she would rather be doing, which would increase the amount of distraction she experienced. This makes tasks take even longer, which would throw her entire schedule off if she had a list of things she needed to do that day.

- Connecting ideas

One of the ways that make memory easier is by connecting ideas that lead us to the information our brain seeks; however, that is much harder for our sons and daughters with ADHD.

Unfortunately, working memory is one of the main impairments your son or daughter suffers from because of their ADHD. This working memory is a huge part of their executive functioning that you are, by now, getting to be an expert on.

The *Journal of Clinical Medicine* recently published a study that compared the effects of acute and chronic exercise on memory function. (Acute exercise is defined as one single session of exercise. Chronic exercise, on the other hand, is repeated sessions of exercise—what I'm referring to as hyperactivity.) The study indicated that hyperactivity (or chronic exercise) increased memory performance, whereas the single exercise sessions showed a significantly lower improvement for the study participants. This technique is complex, though, because the results varied based on when the activity was performed.[41] So, if you want to implement this into your treatment plan, I highly recommend coordinating with your teen's therapist to come up with the best plan for their lifestyle.

---

[41] Loprinzi, P. D., Roig, M., Etnier, J. L., Tomporowski, P. D., & Voss, M. (2021). Acute and Chronic Exercise Effects on Human Memory: What We Know and Where to Go from Here. *Journal of clinical medicine*, 10(21), 4812. https://doi.org/10.3390/jcm10214812.

Regular Exercise

Anyone who exercises receives a boost to their bodies and minds through their endorphins, which send out pain relief and feelings of pleasure when they are released. However, for our children with ADHD, regular exercise can offer even more benefits to their underdeveloped brains.

Kerri Golding, a social worker specializing in working with adolescents diagnosed with ADHD, believes that "exercise does for the brain the same thing that the medications do." The challenge, though, is that the effects do not last as long as medication does.[42]

So, when you combine the medication — if that is a part of your son or daughter's treatment — with regular exercise, you will see improvement in the following areas affected by ADHD:[43]

---

[42] Stewart, Kristen. (2013, December 16). How Exercise Works Like a Drug for ADHD. *Everyday Health.* https://www.everydayhealth.com/add-adhd/can-you-exercise-away-adhd-symptoms.aspx.

[43] 5 Ways Exercise Helps People with ADHD and Autism. (n.d.). Special Strong. Accessed on March 8, 2023, from https://www.specialstrong.com/5-ways-exercise-helps-people-with-adhd-and-autism/.

- Exercise increases dopamine.

  Dopamine is the chemical in your brain that makes you feel good through a neurological reward system. We discussed earlier in the book that the dopamine problem in your teen with ADHD is rather complex. They have a larger number of dopamine transmitters than non-disordered brains. Since these transmitters remove dopamine from the brain, your child has dopamine leaving their brains at higher levels. Essentially, this excess activity from the transmitters lowers the amount of dopamine their brains have access to because they are hyperactive. However, regular exercise can help counteract this process by giving them a larger supply of dopamine to make up for that hyperactive removal process. In addition to improving their ADHD symptoms, this will also benefit them if they experience anxiety, depression, or other mental disorders because they will also be improved by receiving more dopamine. Your son or daughter can choose from various activities to increase their dopamine, such as yoga, walking on a treadmill, weightlifting, sports, walking outside, etc.

- Exercise balances norepinephrine.

Norepinephrine is one of the hormones responsible for the fight-or-flight response of your central nervous system. Whenever your child is feeling stressed for whatever reason, this hormone is the thing that protects them from further harm by directing them to either stand up for themselves (fight) or leave the situation (flight). Consequently, it is also found in dopamine, which we already know is something your son or daughter does not have much of because of their ADHD. However, regular exercise will help them tremendously if their norepinephrine is imbalanced. This means, biologically, they will have more tools to fight the stress they experience daily. This will make them physically healthier and help them manage the stress they experience in social situations, at home, and in the classroom. Though it will not act as a miracle cure — just like any other treatment method I have suggested — it will help improve the symptoms the ADHD medication does not affect.

- Exercise centers on the cerebellum.

The cerebellum is the part of the brain responsible for coordinating movement and balance. The cerebellum is the culprit whenever your child fidgets in their seat, taps their feet, or moves around to release nervous energy. Additionally, researchers are doing much more research on the cerebellum's role in ADHD. They have learned that it is also responsible for the "cognitive processing of emotions and negative stimulus, executive function, and attention and language."[44] In other words, any positive effect your son or daughter receives from regular exercise is going to improve their ADHD symptoms overall because an underdeveloped or unbalanced cerebellum is responsible for the majority of these symptoms. When you combine this with the additional dopamine and balancing of norepinephrine, their ADHD symptoms are being worked on from all points. This fact reinforces why many doctors and researchers believe regular exercise is as effective as ADHD medication. If it was not for the minor detail that the effects do not last as

---

[44] Ding, L., & Pang, G. (2021). Identification of brain regions with enhanced functional connectivity with the cerebellum region in children with attention deficit hyperactivity disorder: A resting-state fmri study. *International Journal of General Medicine, Volume 14,* 2109–2115. https://doi.org/10.2147/ijgm.s303339.

long, they might not even need the medication at all.

- Exercise lessens medication side effects.

Let's face it. The side effects of ADHD medication can be alarming and frustrating, and it might make you wonder at times why anyone would want to take it in the first place. However disrupting those side effects might sound to you, ADHD is even more problematic for your teenager. This often makes it a necessary evil if your child is experiencing some harsh side effects from time to time. However, with a consistent exercise routine, many of these side effects can be eliminated — or at least improved upon. For instance, once my daughter started exercising regularly, we noticed that it counteracted her low appetite and helped her maintain a healthy weight. And over time, we also noticed her sleep quality improving because her meds made getting a good night's sleep more challenging than her ADHD alone. Working together with the increased dopamine, her exercise routine also helped her regulate her mood swings that were not always helped by the medication alone.

- Exercise improves motor skills.

One of the challenges with ADHD that we have not discussed yet is the development of your teen's fine motor skills. These are the skills they need to control the movement of their muscles in their wrists and hands. Because this is one of the areas greatly affected by ADHD, they need some help developing those, and regular exercise can help your son or daughter improve those skills. Simple exercises can help this underdeveloped area; for instance, you can try playing catch or kicking a ball back and forth with your child to help them work on those fine motor skills.

Web Tool for Prescribing Medication

Though this is not a tool you will use along the way, you can still benefit from your psychiatrist or pediatrician using it. When first diagnosed, your teen's doctor likely started with the standard stimulant-based prescription unless they have any other conditions that made them a bad candidate for stimulants. Starting with medications that have delivered results repeatedly is common practice for mental disorders in general. Doctors typically begin with the one they have seen the best results with, then look for other options if their preferred medication does not work for your teenager. (There are also other factors, such as the patient's age, past experience with the medication, allergies, other mental disorders present, insurance approval, etc.)

However, the typical medications do not work for every patient because your child's brain and biological makeup will differ from my daughter's. This is where these software tools or websites can come in and make the process much easier for the doctor and the patient. It removes the one-size-fits-most approach and allows them to find other options that might suit your daughter or son better.

So, if you have been challenged with medications that have not worked, I highly recommend you talk to your doctor about these tools to see if they can help you find better medication options. It could shorten the process by several months and give you peace of mind that your child is getting the best option for them.

Genetic Testing for ADHD Medication

If you have tried everything with undesirable results, genetic testing is an option that has become more commonplace today. With the popularity of DNA testing for ancestry, that field of science has opened up to offer testing for many other things. Some examples include testing for hereditary disorders, dog and cat species and health information, predisposition to certain diseases or disorders, and more. They even use ancestral DNA to find and apprehend criminals by working through family trees.

Today, countless companies do genetic testing that can tell you the best medications based on your DNA. This can help mental health practitioners find a quicker path to the medication that will most likely work for your daughter or son.

Just like your body metabolizes the food you eat, it also goes through the same biological process when you take prescription medication. Your genetic makeup will influence this, which is why it is so important to stay the course when you are having some challenges finding the right medication for your child.

Clarity, one of the companies that do genetic testing for patients, explains how this works on their website:

Different combinations of [your DNA] signify the instructions your genes use to produce proteins in the body.

Proteins are made up of amino acids sequenced from a corresponding gene. Proteins carry out many different functions in the body, and one of those functions is the breakdown (metabolization) of medications. The presence of genetic variations in the genes can impact the instructions needed to produce these enzymes, affecting how individuals respond to medication … When an enzyme reacts too quickly, the drug does not have the chance to be effective. Conversely, when it reacts too slowly, the drug is left in the body and causes harmful side effects.[45]

Though many companies, like Clarity, offer this genetic testing to consumers like you and me, you do not have to do this on your own. Doctors can also order labs that test how your son or daughter's genes react to certain medications. Because these tests can often be expensive, I recommend checking with your insurance company first, so you know what to expect when you go to the appointment.

Prescription Video Games

It is a new world out there. When some of us were children, technology and video games were not nearly as

---

[45] Genetic Testing for ADHD. (n.d.). Clarity. Accessed on March 9, 2023, from https://clarityxdna.com/blog/learn/genetic-testing-for-adhd/.

commonplace as they are today. But, for our kids, these technologies are a normal part of life. However, some video games released for teenagers today can be alarming, as they feature weapons, violence, criminal activity, and many scary creatures. But there's a whole other side to the possibilities of these video games — they can treat ADHD.

These therapeutic video games are unlike their counterparts, often creating nightmares and bad habits in our children. Enter EndeavorRx©. Back in 2020, the Food and Drug Administration (FDA) approved their prescriptive video game as a treatment for ADHD in adolescents between the ages of eight and twelve. The FDA said in a press release: "EndeavorRx is indicated to improve attention function as measured by computed-based testing and is the first digital therapeutic intended to improve symptoms associated with ADHD."[46] And, at the time of this book release, EndeavorRx is still the only FDA-approved therapeutic video game on the market.

The game was created with the help of a neuroscientist

[46] FDA Permits Marketing of First Game-Based Digital Therapeutic to Improve Function in Children with ADHD. (2020, June 15). U.S. Food & Drug. https://www.fda.gov/news-events/press-announcements/fda-permits-marketing-first-game-based-digital-therapeutic-improve-attention-function-children-adhd.

(Adam Gazzaley) and an art director (Matt Omernick), who are two of the founders of this innovative company. This technology has been in the works for quite some time, and it went through seven years of clinical trials before it was submitted to the FDA for approval.[47]

EndeavorRx is not a normal video game, and it especially differentiates itself from the ones your teenager plays regularly. Backed by the FDA's approval, this is how the game works to improve ADHD symptoms: "[It] uses sensory stimuli and motor challenges to target the part of the brain that plays a key role in attention function; as children play over time, algorithms adapt to their progress and personalize the treatment."[48] (You can watch an official trailer of the game here: https://youtu.be/vtCp7JrS9-w.)

Keep in mind, too, that this form of treatment is by prescription only. So, if this sounds like something that might work for your son or daughter, I encourage you to chat with your psychiatrist about getting a prescription.

---

[47] America's Greatest Disruptors: Fun & Gamers. (2021, December 15). *Newsweek.* https://www.newsweek.com/2021/12/24/americas-greatest-disruptors-fun-gamers-1659088.html.

[48] Ibid.

Nerve Stimulation Devices

Technology has more to offer our children with ADHD than innovative video games. Back in 2019, the FDA also approved the use of another technology that has shown improvement in pediatric patients. The eTNS system is an electronic device that works at night while the patient sleeps, delivering low levels of an electric current to the trigeminal nerve for eight hours. The APA reported it had shown around 31 percent improvement in the clinical study of patients who used the device.[49]

Though the trigeminal nerve is responsible for delivering information about physical pain and temperature throughout our body, it also sends blood flow to the other parts of the brain that control focus, attention, emotion, and behavior.[50] This essentially improves the functioning of those areas of your son or daughter's brain that are

---

[49] Greenbaum, Zara. (2019, August). A new device for treating ADHD in children. *Monitor on Psychology.* https://www.apa.org/monitor/2019/07-08/adhd-children.

[50] New Device May Decrease Symptoms. (2019, May 2). *ADHD Weekly.* https://chadd.org/adhd-weekly/new-device-may-decrease-symptoms-without-medication/.

underdeveloped due to their ADHD.

Since the device's approval is fairly new, the cost might be a deciding factor in whether this is a viable option for your teen or not. However, I recommend looking into it before you make your final decision.

* * *

Though some of these options might be out of reach for a wide variety of reasons (age of your child, cost, availability, etc.), it tells us something very promising about our children's futures:

Their struggles with ADHD will have promising solutions tomorrow.

Doctors, scientists, and researchers are working on these solutions every day to improve the lives of our sons and daughters. Though it might feel disheartening, in the beginning, to realize this disorder will be with them their whole lives, their symptoms will evolve and improve, and more and more treatment methods will be available as they grow older.

The work we do today to reclaim the daughters and sons we thought we lost will continue... And, yes, they will live happy and successful lives. ADHD might challenge them and sometimes make it impossible to keep up with their peers, but there is so much hope for a bright future for them.

Conclusion:

I Understand My Teen with ADHD

After all the work we have done, I found my daughter. I can see and appreciate her humor. I can see and appreciate her empathy. I can see and appreciate her need to be liked and valued. Even better, if I do see her anger, I understand that anger. If I do see her anxiety, I understand that anxiety. If I do see her frustration, I understand her frustration. I now know who to talk to if her symptoms get out of control again. I know how to get back on track. My life as a parent of a teen is no longer terrifying. My life as a parent of a teen is no longer confusing. I know who she really is, and she is amazing.

Having a teen with ADHD does not mean that you have lost that child for good. Yes, life is not as easy as it once was, but it is still promising. Opportunities for your child still abound. Don't give up. If something doesn't work, try something else. Don't give up because treatment is there for your teen.

If you need a refresher on the techniques I offered throughout this book, here is a guide that summarizes them for easy reference:

Chapter 1: Who Are You Again?

How to Improve Social Skills

- Take turns practicing social skills.
- Offer several examples for conflict resolution.
- Create scripts for positive social interaction.
- Show them what positive social behavior looks like.

How to Work on Emotional Regulation

- Make a list of coping skills.
- Acknowledge your teen's emotions.
- Introduce healthy habits into your teen's lifestyle.
- Manage your own stress, anxiety, and anger.

Chapter 2: What Is Happening to You?

How to Manage ADHD Symptoms

- Give them time and space to strategize.
- Create an ADHD tool kit.

- Encourage relaxation and decompression.
- Teach them to take care of their body.
- Build their self-esteem.
- Ask for help.

Chapter 3: Why Are You Acting Out?

How to Talk to Your Teen About Addiction and Self-Harm

- Offer your teenager a safe space to talk about their problems.
- Listen to what your child is saying without passing judgment.
- Prepare yourself to hear the hard things.
- Recognize their behavior and lead them in a calm discussion about it.
- Ask for help when you need it.

Other Ways to Help Your Addicted and/or Self-Harming Teenager

- Advocate for their diagnosis of late-onset ADHD.
- Research and ask questions to alleviate your concerns.
- Offer your son or daughter love, understanding, and patience.

Chapter 4: How Can I Help You with School?

Possible Accommodations to Discuss with Your Teen's Support Team at School

• Sit the student near a good role model.

• Break long assignments into smaller parts or shorten the assignments.

• Allow extra time to complete assigned work.

• Pair written instructions with oral instructions.

• Ask the student questions to allow them to participate in the class discussion.

• Involve the student in planning the lessons to engage them in their education.

• Set up a private signal with the teacher that tells the student to pay attention without embarrassing them.

• Schedule a five-minute meeting before turning in homework or tests to go over their work.

• Ignore minor inappropriate behavior.

• Increase immediacy of rewards and consequences.

• Acknowledge correct answers only when they raise

their hand and are called upon.

- Send daily or weekly progress reports
- Set up a behavior contract
- Recommend binders with dividers and folders for organization
- Supervise writing down of assignments
- Allow student to keep a set of books at home to help with forgetfulness
- Invite student to run errands if they are acting restless
- Provide short breaks between assignments
- Set up social behavior goals with student and implement rewards
- Encourage cooperative learning tasks
- Assign special responsibilities in social peer groups
- Compliment positive behavior to help build their leadership skills
- Encourage socializing with classmates
- Acknowledge appropriate behavior and good work frequently
- Encourage student to walk away when they are angry

Chapter 5: Are Your Friends a Good Influence on You?

Attributes of a Positive Influence

- Positive attitude
- Inclusive of others
- Encourages healthy extracurricular activities

How to Navigate Away from a Negative Influence

- Develop willpower.
- Define healthy habits.
- Find treatment for addiction.

Possible Extracurricular Activities

- Subject-related after-school groups (French Club, Debate Club, Science Club, etc.)
- Clubs that would challenge her intellectually (like Chess Club)
- School Sports
- Journalism (newspaper staff or the yearbook)
- Electives that would inspire her artistic side (photography, visual art, drama, etc.)
- Girl Scouts

Healthy Habits to Replace Addictive Behavior

- Drawing, writing, photography, or some other artistic pursuit

- Playing chess, cards, or board games with friends or family members
- Reading on an interesting subject
- Going online (or to the library) to research career options
- Taking a family trip to the zoo, museum, art gallery, the movies, or a convention
- Walking around the block, doing yoga, lifting weights, or dancing to boost endorphins
- Watching a funny movie or television show
- Writing feelings down in a journal, then talking about them together
- Doing fun chores around the house
- Working on homework together
- Calling a friend to hang out
- Learning something new and interesting
- Going shopping for a new outfit, game, or book to reward continued sobriety

Some Gentle Reminders When Dealing with Addiction

- It is not your fault that your teen got addicted.
- It is also not your child's fault.
- Enabling your teenager can make things worse.

- Harsh punishment will not help your child stay clean, either.
- Pain lies at the root of addiction.
- Your child has to choose recovery.
- They will need a lot of support.
- Sobriety does not happen overnight.
- They might say things they do not mean.
- It only takes a brief moment to slip.
- Your teen's relapse does not mean they failed.
- You can not do everything for them.
- You need to take care of yourself too.

Chapter 6: How Can I Help You Find Treatment?

Therapeutic Journaling Prompts

- If you could go anywhere in the world right now, where would you be, and why?
- Is there anyone with whom you feel you can be your full self unapologetically? Who is this person, and what about them makes you feel so free?
- Is there a dream or a nightmare that you have over and over again? Without looking it up, what do you personally think it means?
- What is the thing you fear the most in the world? Do

you think this fear is valid? What does it stop you from doing? What would you do differently if you didn't have this fear?

- Have you cried happy tears? What made it happen? Why do you think it affected you that way?

- Is there a song lyric that really motivates you and helps you push through difficult times? What's the lyric? How does it inspire you?

- Is there a lie you've told recently that you regret? Why did you tell it? Who did you lie to? What would have happened if you had told the truth?

- What have you said yes to recently that you wished you had said no to? What stopped you from saying no?

- What does unconditional love mean to you?

- Who do you admire the most in the world and why?

Eight-Step Problem-Solving Process

1. Define the problem.
2. Clarify the problem.
3. Define the goal.
4. Identify the root cause of the problem.
5. Develop an action plan.
6. Execute action plan.

7. Evaluate the results.

8. Continuously improve.

Methods for Managing Behavior

- Start with goals the child can achieve in small steps.
- Be consistent across different times of the day, different settings, and different people.
- Provide consequences immediately following behavior.
- Implement behavioral interventions over the long haul, not just for a few months.

Chapter 7: Can I Talk to You About ADHD?

How to Find Success with Therapy

- Research online to find the right professionals.
- Make sure your child is comfortable.
- Commit to going to therapy regularly.
- Follow through with the treatment plan.

Attributes of a Good Mental Health Practitioner (for Parents)

- Experience with ADHD
- Experience with teenagers
- Empathy

- Proven results

Attributes of a Good Mental Health Practitioner (for Teens)

- They will give them space to express themselves without judging them.
- They will listen attentively.
- They will be trustworthy and show they care.
- They will have good techniques for improving academic performance.
- They will understand that some subjects are hard to talk about.

How to Support Your Teen's Therapy Journey

- Be available if they need to talk.
- Encourage positive self-talk.
- Support and encourage them in their treatment plan.
- Give them their privacy.
- Check-in to see how their therapy is going.
- Be willing to participate genuinely in therapy sessions.

Before we say goodbye, I hope our time together has helped you understand your teenager better and given you various coping techniques to help them with their ADHD. If you enjoyed this book, I would love it if you would leave a review on Amazon to help other moms and dads like you find the help they need.

Good luck with the rest of your therapeutic journey!

References

ADHD Quick Facts: Behavior Management in ADHD Treatment. (n.d.). CHADD. Accessed March 4, 2023, from https://chadd.org/about-adhd/adhd-quick-facts-behavior-management-in-adhd-treatment/.

Ali, S., Mouton, C. P., Jabeen, S., Ofoemezie, E. K., Bailey, R. K., Shahid, M., & Zeng, Q. (2011). Early detection of illicit drug use in teenagers. *Innovations in clinical neuroscience*, *8*(12), 24–28.

America's Greatest Disruptors: Fun & Gamers. (2021, December 15). *Newsweek.* https://www.newsweek.com/2021/12/24/americas-greatest-disruptors-fun-gamers-1659088.html.

American Psychiatric Association. (2013). *Diagnostic and Statistical Manual of Mental Disorders (5th ed.).* https://doi.org/10.1176/appi.books.9780890425596.

Breaux, Rosanna, PhD. (2020). Emotional Regulation in Teens with ADHD. CHADD. https://chadd.org/adhd-news/adhd-news-caregivers/emotion-regulation-in-teens-with-adhd/.

Breus, Michael, Ph.D. (2022, December 13). ADHD and Sleep. The Sleep Doctor. https://thesleepdoctor.com/mental-health/adhd-and-sleep/.

Carpenter, Siri. (2001, May). Stimulants boost achievement in ADHD teens. *Monitor on Psychology.* https://www.apa.org/monitor/may01/stimulants.

Chang, Z., Lichtenstein, P., Halldner, L., D'Onofrio, B., Serlachius, E., Fazel, S., Långström, N., & Larsson, H. (2013). Stimulant ADHD medication and risk for substance abuse. *Journal of Child Psychology and Psychiatry, 55*(8), 878–885. https://doi.org/10.1111/jcpp.12164.

Ding, L., & Pang, G. (2021). Identification of brain regions with enhanced functional connectivity with the cerebellum region in children with attention deficit hyperactivity disorder: A resting-state fmri study. *International Journal of General Medicine, Volume 14,* 2109–2115. https://doi.org/10.2147/ijgm.s303339.

8-Step Problem-Solving Process. (n.d.) University of Iowa. Accessed March 4, 2023, from https://hr.uiowa.edu/development/organizational-development/lean/8-step-problem-solving-process.

Executive Function. (n.d.). *Psychology Today.* Retrieved February 18, 2023, from https://www.psychologytoday.com/us/basics/executive-function.

FDA Permits Marketing of First Game-Based Digital Therapeutic to Improve Function in Children with ADHD. (2020, June 15). U.S. Food & Drug. https://www.fda.gov/news-events/press-announcements/fda-permits-marketing-first-game-based-digital-therapeutic-improve-attention-function-children-adhd.

5 Ways Exercise Helps People with ADHD and Autism. (n.d.). Special Strong. Accessed on March 8, 2023, from https://www.specialstrong.com/5-ways-exercise-helps-people-with-adhd-and-autism/.

Genetic Testing for ADHD. (n.d.). Clarity. Accessed on March 9, 2023, from https://clarityxdna.com/blog/learn/genetic-testing-for-adhd/.

Goldstein, Sam, Ph.D. (n.d.). What Is the Relationship Between ADHD and Self-Control? LD Online. Accessed February 23, 2023, from https://www.ldonline.org/ld-topics/behavior-social-skills/what-relationship-between-adhd-and-self-control.

Greenbaum, Zara. (2019, August). A new device for treating ADHD in children. *Monitor on Psychology.* https://www.apa.org/monitor/2019/07-08/adhd-children.

Guerreiro, D. F., Figueira, M. L., Cruz, D., & Sampaio, D. (2015). Coping strategies in adolescents who self-harm. *Crisis,* *36*(1), 31–37. https://doi.org/10.1027/0227-5910/a000289.

Helping Girls With ADHD Make Friends. (2021, August 19). Child Mind Institute. https://childmind.org/article/helping-girls-with-adhd-make-friends/.

How ADHD Contributes to Memory Problems. (n.d.). THINK Neurology for Kids. Accessed on March 8, 2023, from https://www.thinkkids.com/blog/how-adhd-contributes-to-memory-problems.

How To Support Your Teen Through Therapy. (n.d.). Ashley Therapy. Accessed on March 6, 2023, from https://www.ashleytreatment.org/rehab-blog/support-teens-therapy/.

Juby, Bethany, PsyD. (2021, August 17). Tips for Coping with ADHD. https://psychcentral.com/adhd/best-tips-for-coping-with-adhd.

Launder, Amy. (2020, April 30). 20 Therapeutic Journal Prompts. https://www.amylaunder.com/blog/20-therapeutic-journal-prompts.

Legg, Timothy, J., Ph.D., PsyD. (2019, June 18). What is the link between ADHD and dopamine? *Medical News Today.* https://www.medicalnewstoday.com/articles/325499.

Loprinzi, P. D., Roig, M., Etnier, J. L., Tomporowski, P. D., & Voss, M. (2021). Acute and Chronic Exercise Effects on Human Memory: What We Know and Where to Go from Here. *Journal of clinical medicine*, *10*(21), 4812. https://doi.org/10.3390/jcm10214812.

Miller, Caroline. (2023, January 9). Social Issues for Kids With Learning Problems. Child Mind Institute. https://childmind.org/article/social-challenges-kids-learning-problems/.

Miller, Caroline. (2023, January 26). What Are Non-stimulant Medications for ADHD? Child Mind Institute. https://childmind.org/article/what-are-nonstimulant-medications-for-adhd/.

New Device May Decrease Symptoms. (2019, May 2). *ADHD Weekly.* https://chadd.org/adhd-weekly/new-device-may-decrease-symptoms-without-medication/.

Nigg, Joel, Ph.D. (2022, July 11). Anger Issues and ADHD. *ADDitude*. https://www.additudemag.com/anger-issues-adhd-emotional-dysregulation/.

Novotney, Amy. (2019, May). The risks of social isolation. *Monitor on Psychology*. https://www.apa.org/monitor/2019/05/ce-corner-isolation.

Saline, Sharon, Psy.D. (2022, March 31). Anxiety in Teens with ADHD. *ADDitude*. https://www.additudemag.com/anxiety-in-teens-adhd-reframing-skills/.

Seay, Bob. (2022, October 28). Accommodations to Include in Your Child's IEP. *ADDitude*. https://www.additudemag.com/20-adhd-accommodations-that-work/.

Self-Control. (n.d.). *Psychology Today*. Accessed February 19, 2023, from https://www.psychologytoday.com/us/basics/self-control.

Signs and Risk Factors of Self-Harm in Youth. (2022, January 28). Camber Children's Mental Health. https://www.cambermentalhealth.org/2022/01/28/signs-and-risks-of-self-harm-in-youth/.

Singh, I. (2011). A disorder of anger and aggression: children's perspectives on attention-deficit/hyperactivity disorder in the UK. *Social science & medicine (1982)*, 73(6), 889–896. https://doi.org/10.1016/j.socscimed.2011.03.049.

Stewart, Kristen. (2013, December 16). How Exercise Works Like a Drug for ADHD. *Everyday Health.* https://www.everydayhealth.com/add-adhd/can-you-exercise-away-adhd-symptoms.aspx.

The Global Misdiagnosis of ADHD and the Devastating Long-Term Effects. (2021, August 11). *Pre-Collegiate Global Health Review.* https://www.pghr.org/post/the-global-misdiagnosis-of-adhd-and-the-devastating-long-term-effects.

13 Things to Understand About Teen Substance Abuse. (n.d.). Safe Landing. Accessed on March 3, 2023, from https://www.safelandingrecovery.com/blog/13-things-parents-dont-get-about-teen-substance-abuse/.

Turgay, A., & Ansari, R. (2006). Major Depression with ADHD: In Children and Adolescents. *Psychiatry (Edgmont (Pa.: Township))*, 3(4), 20–32.

Van der Oord, S., & Tripp, G. (2020). How to Improve Behavioral Parent and Teacher Training for Children with ADHD: Integrating Empirical Research on Learning and Motivation into Treatment. *Clinical child and family psychology review*, 23(4), 577–604. https://doi.org/10.1007/s10567-020-00327-z.

Warning Signs of Self-Harm. (n.d.) Ball State University. Accessed on February 28, 2023, from https://www.bsu.edu/campuslife/healthsafety/campus-safety/campussafetyhandbook/warningsignsofselfharm.

What is Dopamine? (n.d.) Mental Health America. Accessed on February 25, 2023, from https://mhanational.org/what-dopamine.

Made in United States
North Haven, CT
29 October 2024

59582365R00108